HUMAN RESOURCE DEVELOPMENT For The Food Industries

by

Wilbur A. Gould, Ph. D.

Food Industries Consultant,

Executive Director
Mid-America Food Processors Association,

and

Emeritus Professor
Food Processing and Technology
The Ohio State University

Human Resource Development For The Food Industries

Printed and bound by CPI Group (UK) Ltd, Croydon, CR0 4YY

ISBN Numbers are as follows: 0-930027-22-1

Library of Congress Cataloging - in - Publication Data

Gould, Wilbur A., 1920-
Human Resource Development For The Food Industries / by Wilbur A. Gould.
p. cm..
Includes bibliographical references and index.
ISBN 0-930027-22-1
1. Food Industry and trade - United States - Personnel management
2. Food industry and trade - United States - Management.
3. Labor laws and legislation - United States. I. Title.
HD9005.G68 1994 94-15330
664'.0068'3-dc20 CIP

CTI PUBLICATIONS Inc.

2619 Maryland Ave., Baltimore, MD 21218-4547 USA

410-467-3338 FAX 410/467/7434

This Copy Of

Human Resource Development For The Food Industries

Belongs to:

ABOUT THE AUTHOR

Wilbur A. Gould was reared on a farm in Northern New Hampshire. He received his Bachelor of Science degree from the University of New Hampshire in Horticulture-Plant Breeding. He started his graduate work at Michigan State University prior to service in the U.S. Navy during World War II. After military service, he completed his Master of Science and Ph.D degrees at The Ohio State University.

Dr. Gould retired from The Ohio State University after 39 years on the faculty as Professor of Food Processing and Technology. He taught 9 courses during his tenure and advised over 900 undergraduate students, 131 Master of Science Students and 76 Doctoral students. His major research interests were in Vegetable Processing and Technology and Snack Food Manufacture and Quality Assurance. He has authored some 83 referred journal research publications, over 200 Food Trade articles, and 10 books.

Dr. Gould is a Member of Phi Kappa Phi, Phi Sigma, Phi Tau Sigma, Sigma Xi, Gamma Sigma Delta (Award of Merit in 1984), Alpha Gamma Rho, Institute of Food Technologists (Fellow in 1982), and American Society of Horticultural Science (Distinguished Graduate Teaching Award in 1985).

The following are some of the recognitions that Dr. Gould has received: The Ohio State University Distinguished Leadership to Students Award in 1963 and a Certificate of Recognition Award in 1986; Ohio Food Processors H.D. Brown Person of Year Award in 1971; Ohio Food Processors Association Tomato Achievement Award in 1985; Ozark Food Processors Association Outstanding Professional Leadership Award in 1978; 49er's Service Award in 1979; Food Processing Machinery and Supplies Association Leadership and Service Award in 1988; Ohio

Agricultural Hall of Fame in 1989, an Honorary Life Membership in Potato Association of America in 1990, and was the Institute of Food Technologist's 1993 Nicholas Appert Award Medalist.

Dr. Gould presently serves as Executive Director of Mid-America Food Processors Association, Food Technology Consultant to the Snack Food Association, Secretary-Treasurer of The Guard Society, and Consultant to the Food Industries.

Dr. Gould's philosophy is to tell it as he sees it, be short and get right to the point.

PREFACE

People are the greatest resource any firm has and how we utilize this resource is most important for the success of the food firm.

People in a food firm are as different as you and I. This is only natural. It is impossible to clone the people in a firm and have them all act and react as someone might think they should. The handling of these differences are most significant in the full utilization of this great resource.

All my life I have worked with people. I started on the farm working with my brothers and the other farm help. I advanced this working relationship through Colebrook Academy where I became President of my class and much involved in sports. This was carried further as I played Lacrosse at the University of New Hampshire and I scored the only goal when we played Harvard. In the Navy I was the Squadron Leader at Boot Camp at Sampson Naval Base and eventually became the Petty Officer responsible for the Food Supply in the 14th Naval District during World War II.

Since World War II, I have worked with Little Leaguers with some 700 youngsters during the two years that I served as Commissioner. I worked with the citizens of Worthington as a City Councilman for two years and worked on the present city programs of development. At The Ohio State University, I taught nine course annually with enrollments in my class exceeding some 50 students per course and I had the privilege of advising over 1100 students in my 39 year tenure. Today, many of my former students are the leaders in this great industry. During much of this same time I have had the pleasure of working with the food processing industry in Mid-america as their Association Executive Officer for some 40 years.

Working with people has taught me humbleness, taught me sympathy, taught me responsibility, taught me leadership, taught me to care and love, and taught me to be forgiving. I am sincerely thankful for all the opportunities that have come my way. I am greatly appreciative for what it has meant to me as a teacher, coach, leader, trainer, and coordinator. I am grateful for the wonderful people who have touched my life and I honestly can say that the time and effort that I have given has been all the reward one could ever hope for.

Every endeavor has involved a commingling of people. They are wonderful and I am most proud when I observe their growth, relish in their accomplishments, and see the fulfillment of their dreams. People are our greatest asset and my hope is that every reader of this book will find relevance as they work with this great resource.

Wilbur A. Gould, Ph. D.

ACKNOWLEDGEMENTS

I am deeply indebted to given segments of the food industries for the privilege of participating in lectures, consultations, and workshops dealing with various facets of human resources. These opportunities have afforded me a laboratory to develop experience in working with people and the development of the many aspects of human resources.

My most sincere thanks to my former colleagues and students at The Ohio State University for their encouragement and insights. I thank the many food processors I have worked with on the development of their human resources.

I wish to sincerely thank Ron Gould for his untiring help, his enthusiastic interest, and his full cooperation in keeping me on the right plateau when dealing with the whole subject of human resources. He has been an indispensable source of help.

I also wish to thank Steve Wheeler, Human Resources Consultant, Wheeler & Associates, 3755 Dance Mill Rd., Phoenix, MD 21131, 410-592-3552, for his kind contribution to this manuscipt. Steve brought the angle of law into play in relation to the Human Resource function.

I especially wish to thank Jessie Gould, Art Judge, II, and Randy Gerstmyer for their wholehearted encouragement during the formatting, writing, editing, and publication of this manuscript. Because of their interest and support, I hope this book is complete and that it becomes most useful to all concerned.

I dedicate this book to all those in this great industry, whether they be the leader, the employee, or the human resource person. The future is in your hands as you work toward the goal. Each of you can make the difference and you all can become winners.

Wilbur A. Gould

HUMAN RESOURCE DEVELOPMENT
For The Food Industries

by
Wilbur A. Gould

TABLE OF CONTENTS

TABLE OF CONTENTS Continued

CHAPTER 1

IMPROVEMENT OF HUMAN RESOURCES FOR THE FOOD INDUSTRIES

INTRODUCTION

"When you win, nothing hurts." Joe Namath

Human resources in the food industries or any industry or any business is without question the first criteria for success. People make a company or firm. People are the 'cog' that keeps the firm running. People are the most underutilized aspect of most businesses. Too many times people are taken for granted and often treated as numbers not as individuals.

The development of human resources is a major aspect of any food business. Human resource development can reduce the human variability in the firm. Human resource development can improve productivity. Human resource development can better assure product quality. Human resource development can significantly improve efficiency. Most importantly, human resource development can improve customer relations.

How we recruit our personnel, how we train our personnel, and how we work with our personnel are all major factors in the development of human resources. If we develop our people along with our process, our methods, and our products, we should see major improvements in the success of the food firm.

Everyone likes to be called by their first name and everyone likes to feel important. Everyone likes to have known responsibilities and everyone likes to be recognized for achievement. Further, everyone wants to be challenged or given opportunities to show their abilities. I, also, believe everyone wants to be treated fairly and given an opportunity to excel in their area of expertise or ability. If one doubts this, all one has to do is to watch TV and note the characters playing out their role whether it be a sitcom, comedy, musical, sport, or even the news reader. They are living out their role and doing their thing. Individual accomplishment is a great thing and it should be recognized. Forms of recognition are many and they are important, at least, from an ego standpoint and we all really want to be recognized for our efforts.

This book is all about being a coach, the individual worker and how to be a better team player. I have set forth here some thoughts from experience and trial and error methods that, hopefully, will be helpful to the individual, to the leader and the coach or management in achieving greater success in the food industries.

No book is ever complete or full of everything you always wanted to know. My experience is that each book should have something to offer and as we move through life we should gain new experiences with every step along the way. My hope is that this book will be that stepping stone you have been looking for to help you move through life with greater enthusiasm, greater vigor, greater vitality, and greater desire to achieve.

People are our most important asset and as we learn to work together as teams just as major sports team do, our chemistry and our physical and mental relationships should get stronger and better. We quickly learn our weaknesses and our strengths as we work with others of greater or lesser strengths and weaknesses. In reality we should all gain from these experiences and build on each other for the good of the whole. Together we can and we will be better for it and our firm will be the winner in providing products that our customers expect all the time.

The customer will be the ultimate winner and our firm will grow just as we expect to grow with our firm that is on the move to greater heights in efficiencies and productivity and improved quality. You can help yourself and you can make major contributions if you believe in yourself and the contributions that you can make.

CHAPTER 2

CHANGES IN THE FOOD INDUSTRIES

"Top achievers are almost always close to someone who is even more successful than they are. Not only does this person have a broad overview of the industry, he is also willing to share this knowledge to the recipient's benefit." Derkin & Wise, Inc.

The food industry as we know it today is going through significant changes. Many firms are growing, others are merging, and some are loosing ground or going out of business. The life cycle of the industry really is of concern if we are to meet the challenge during the rest of this century and the years that lie in the next century. Food will always be needed as long as man is on the face of this earth. The quality of that food and the cost of the food, in large part is determined by people and the food firms they work for. People are a major variable in everything that happens within the food industry. However, before we get into the sense of this book, we should stop and take a look at the industry and the major players and how they have changed.

Food Industry Life Cycles

The life cycle of food firms follows through four stages. The first of these stages is what some call the formative years, I refer to it as the beginning of an idea by some individual or entrepreneur. It is that time in the life of the food firm when everything is developing including how to do it, why we are doing it, when it should be done, who is going to do what, and where it is going to be done. Many food firms started developing their first product right on Mom's kitchen stove or in the garage or perhaps in a laboratory. The conceived idea was put into form and from that day forward a new firm was born. In many cases it was a very slow start, but hard work and diligent and patient effort made it a success. Over time the new firm grew and established itself as a food firm to be reckoned with. Time, money, and people made it a success.

This new firm matured into a stable growth industry and the products it produced met the expectations of its customers. The mature firm may have added new lines of products, it learned to utilize new and modern methods of manufacture. Further, it grew because the right raw materials were always utilized to satisfy the customer and, most importantly, people made it a continuing success.

The business eventually became an old established firm as it aged along with the ownership or management. Without new "blood" or leadership it lost that drive, that desire, that "get up and go" and eventually this old thriving firm reached the fourth stage in the life cycle of any firm, that is, it would go out of business as such unless a merger or new ownership came to the forefront. Many firms reaching the "demise" stage can come back by infusion of new management, new funds, new ideas, new practices, new products, and new people to get away from the old status quo.

In my opinion there is absolutely no need for a food firm to go out of business in these times if they are staying up with the times in equipment, materials, methodology, human resources, and marketing know-how. This simply means they have to modernize on a regular consistent basis, they must reformulate as the customer changes eating habits, they must become more efficient to meet the competition head on, and they must have forward thinking and empowered personnel to operate with reduced overhead.

Food is the staff of life and the processed food industries should be very proud of its past record in feeding the nation and much of the world. The past is prologue to the future and our leadership should lead by example and not follow in "fathers" footsteps. Leadership in the food industry has been slow to change and slow to recognize that the changes needed are upon us. The following are some paradigm shifts that are most meaningful and should be good as to what we should be all about today.

Mission, Vision, and Values

First and foremost every firm should set forth its mission, vision and value statement. They should share these with all who will listen and read. People want to know the kind of firm they are working for and what vision does management have for the future and most importantly what are the firm's values.

I prepared the information in Figure 2.1 for Mid-America Food Processors Association members and as I travel to the membership I find this carefully framed and precisely placed in the reception area of many of the plants for all to see. This is great, but what must be done is that each firm should carefully communicate this to all the employees and live by this credo. I have read many similar statements from various food and supply firms and I find them most informative and helpful in understanding the firm and its mission, vision and values. These statements are what we stand for and what we are committed to and what we really want to accomplish. To me they are the ultimate in describing a food firm. Hopefully, they are carefully communicated to all who will listen or read.

Some Paradigm Shifts

In past years most food firms were tall and rigid in structure with "layers" of management. The modern trend is that food firms are becoming more flat and flexible and able to move without lengthy meetings to make the necessary changes to keep the firm on the grow. Eliminating layers of management has required the training and empowerment of our people to make the necessary decisions on the spot. This has strengthened the firm and permitted it to act more quickly and responsibly. It has meant that operating individuals have had to assume responsibilities along with their empowerment. After all the operator is the one who should know most about the machine or line they are operating. This shift of responsibility is a major improvement in operating a facility and it should lead to greater efficiencies with improved control of quality and productivity. The most important aspect of this paradigm shift is that the individual line worker must be trained and provided the tools to make the decisions with precision. The elimination of levels of management is a right decision as some layers of management may not always have been tuned in on what the line operator already knows.

This leads to the next paradigm shift and that is command decisions versus consensus decisions. This decision simply means that two heads are better than one and most people today do not respond to commands very favorably. Further, it means that threats and fear are out and control is arrived at by positive reinforcement through consensus action and adequate training to cope with the shift.

Another paradigm shift is that we no longer have experts and labor. Everyone in the modern food plant becomes an expert because we have trained all and we can now empower them and hold every one accountable. The operator generates his or her own data using their "tool" box for interpretation and these data will indicate what is going on at all times and where to pin point the approvements. Records become scores and our empowered people are the actual scorekeeper. The most important thing is they know who is winning at all times and they know what they have to do to compete. They can see every improvement and build efficiency and the 'bottom line' as they go.

Joel Barker concluded a discussion on paradigm shifts with the following story:

"Once upon a time, there was a man who had a cabin in the mountains and a Porsche to get there. Every Saturday morning, he would drive up to his cabin on a very dangerous road filled with blind curves, unguarded drop off, and tricky turns. But this man was not bothered by danger. After all, he had a great car to drive, he was an excellent driver, and he knew the road like the back of his hand. One fine Saturday morning, he was driving to his cabin. He was coming up to one of his favorite blind curves. He slowed down, shifted gears, and put on the brakes in prepara-

tion for the turn that was about two hundred yards away. All of sudden, from around that curve, came a car careening almost out of control! The car nearly went off the cliff but, at the last second, its driver pulled the car back on the road. The car swerved into his lane, than back into its lane, then back into his lane again. My God, he thought, I am going to be hit! So he slowed almost to a stop. The car came racing on toward him, swerving back and forth. Just before it was about to hit him - at the last moment - it swung back into its lane. As it went past him, a beautiful woman stuck her head out the window of the car and yelled at him at the top of her lungs, "PIG!!" What,? he thought, How dare she call me that! He was incensed by her accusation! Instantly he yelled after her, "SOW!!!" as she continued down the road. "I was in my lane! She was the one who was all over the place!" he muttered to himself. Then he began to get control of his rage; he smiled and was pleased that at least she didn't get away without his stinging retort. He'd gotten her good, he thought smugly. And with that, he put the accelerator to the floor and raced around that blind curve....and ran into the pig! This is a paradigm story. He thought the woman was calling him a name. But she was really doing a heroic thing. In spite of the fact that she had almost been killed, she took the time to try to warn him about the pig on the road around the curve. But he had paradigm paralysis. He thought she called him a name; so he followed "the rules" and called her a name...and thought that was the end of it. Actually, he had demonstrated the beginnings of some flexibility when he noticed that it was she, not he, who was swerving all over the road. If he had paradigm pliancy, he would have responded to her shout by asking himself, What is going on? Then he would have driven around the corner much more cautiously. At the least, he would not have hit the pig. At the most, he could have stopped, picked the pig up, put it in his trunk, and driven away with it. The moral: During the next decade many people will be coming around blind curves yelling things at you. They will be too busy to stop and explain, so it will be up to you to figure it out. If you have paradigm paralysis, you will be hearing nothing but threats. If you have paradigm pliancy, you will be hearing nothing but opportunity!"

The choice of making the paradigm shift is entirely up to you, the leader of your firm. **Barker, Joel Arthur. Paradigms**

FIGURE 2.1 - Mission, Vision & Values

Mid-America Food Processors Association

OUR MISSION

To represent the food industry in Middle America and to help the Membership improve their production, processing, marketing, and technological know how using scientific knowledge focusing on identified issues and needs.

Further, to respond to the common needs of our membership by providing information and programs to strengthen their productivity. To provide information to influence positive consumer opinion.

We are dedicated to sound principles and avowed efforts to lead the food industry to greater stature.

OUR VISION

Mid-America Food Processors Association is broadly recognized throughout the industry as a premier educational and technological organization. It is a dynamic association strengthening individuals, firms, and organizations in partnership for the common good of the food industry. We

- ★ Concentrate on critical economical, environmental, safety, and technological issues.
- ★ Promote Current Good Manufacturing Practices.
- ★ Install approved safety devices and programs.
- ★ Sponsor workshops and educational programs.
- ★ Maintain active government relations programs.
- ★ Conduct promotion and PR programs.
- ★ Coordinate efforts of suppliers, governmental agencies and academic centers of excellence.
- ★ Publish informative newsletters and bulletins.
- ★ Provide a forum for exchange of ideas and facts.
- ★ Maintain professional relationships with members, growers, & suppliers.

OUR VALUES

As Members, Associate Members and Growers of Mid-America Food Processors Association, we are dedicated to the following:

→ We believe in an emphasis on excellence.

→ We believe in programs that help all our people solve mutual problems.

→ We believe in the practice of total compliance with all regulations.

→ We believe in working together as an industry for the ultimate good of the consumer, the user of all of our efforts.

→ We believe in the products we manufacture and we will exert our position as a leader in the production, processing and packing of safe, wholesome, high quality, and nutritious foods.

→ We believe in the products we manufacture and we will exert our position as a leader in the production, processing and packing of safe, wholesome, high quality, and nutritious foods.

→ We believe in service, honesty, and integrity in our work and to all our customers.

→ We believe in the philosophy of teamwork and in helping all our people to help themselves.

→ We believe in credibility and absolute product quality control and we assure that all the products we produce, process, pack, and market meet our customers' expectations all the time.

→ We believe in total cooperation and friendly competition with all our competitors for the ultimate benefit of all of our customers.

CHAPTER 3

CAUSES OF VARIATIONS IN FOOD MANUFACTURE

"There are no secrets to success. It is the result of preparation, hard work, learning from failures". General Colin L. Powell

There are five basic causes of variations in a food plant (see Figure 3.1). These are (1) Materials, (2) Machinery, (3) Methods, (4) Manpower or Human Resources, and (5) Environment.

This book is all about Manpower Variation or the variable Human Resources. Human resources is perhaps the most important single variable in a food processing operation that can be improved. Improvement must come from management by supplying the necessary resources to provide personnel that are suitable for the particular operation and to keep them up with the times through continuous education.

To start with, my credo says:

We believe that modern food plants are systems of machines and people making a product and the success of these plants is due entirely to the management of these systems.

We believe that good managers take proper action based on the observations of the worker because the worker is the first to notice changes in the system.

Deming

To back these two statements up one needs to look to leaders like Dr. Edward Deming. He was one of the world class leaders in controlling quality, increasing efficiency, and improving the bottom line. He was a most powerful man in USA and the World and his contributions have changed the way many firms operate today.

Deming states that 80-85% of quality problems are due to design and process inadequacies and poor management. The other 15-20% are due to employees.

Deming believes that if the system does not do what it should, there are two causes: Special causes and Common causes.

Deming further states that common causes can be easily measured, isolated and corrected and that common causes stay in the system until management reduces them.

Deming, also, states that special causes represent 15-20% of the system--they are peculure to either the worker or the machine.

Workers

Since workers work in the system, the worker is the first to observe the cause of problems. Workers know the behavior of the system. Workers observe the details of every-day operation of the system. Workers will develop great pride, enthusiasm and become more effective if given a voice in the operation of the system.

Most leaders agree that, people are our greatest resource. The real question is how do we use this resource?

Theory X

Theory "x" foundation for Theory x is that the worker does not really need to work. He or she must be constantly driven by their superiors. Some say our workers punch in at 8 and out at 5 with little contributions in between.

Theory Y

Theory "y" says that the worker wants to work. The worker wants to plan and control his or her actions to achieve the goals of the firm. Superiors take the role of support for the worker.

People

Thus, if an organization wishes to improve its position within the industry, it must focus on people. People make a company. Decisions and plans are made by people. Work is done by people. In reality, continuous improvement will only be achieved through people.

People, you and I, want from our jobs Money to satisfy basic needs. We want Security to assure ourselves of a future. We want Involvement meaning achievement, that is, sense of purpose, part of a team and part of the organization and not treated just a "gopher". We want Recognition from our peers and our superiors only after we have earned it. We want Challenges to prevent the ho-hum attitude. We want the Authority, the Empowerment, the Responsibilities, and we want to be held Accountable for our work. Yes, we want Opportunity to do what we think should be done. These wants are not out of order and I really believe that is what most workers want from their job.

Therefore, its most important that people understand what is to be done, how it should be done, why it is done a certain way, when it must be done, where it is to be done, and who is to do it. People generally need intense training and help to understand the control of quality and efficiency in productivity. Help must be generated by management for the long term goals of any modern food firm. Help includes the opportunity to study, to learn, to become better educated and schooled in the new, the wondrous, the fascinating, and the ever advancing technology in this great industry.

I really believe employees, that is, the workers would be greatly satisfied with their personal subscription to a trade magazine of their choice, to receive a new book to stimulate their thinking as an annual gift, and to be given an opportunity to attend, at least, one annual outside activity (workshop, meeting, convention, etc.) for their growth and an opportunity to meet with their peers.

Management could really motivate their people and have a much better handle on this variable if an all out effort was made to bring the worker or the employee into the family and make them feel ownership, partnership, and the satisfaction of belonging. Every human resource is too valuable a resource to waste. We must learn to be truthful and have great empathy for each individual in our employ. There really is something good in every one of us and our leaders need to help us to find the good within us. By placing more emphasis on this valuable resource, management can make significant improvement in the productivity and quality of work within the firm.

FIGURE 3.1 - Causes Of Variation

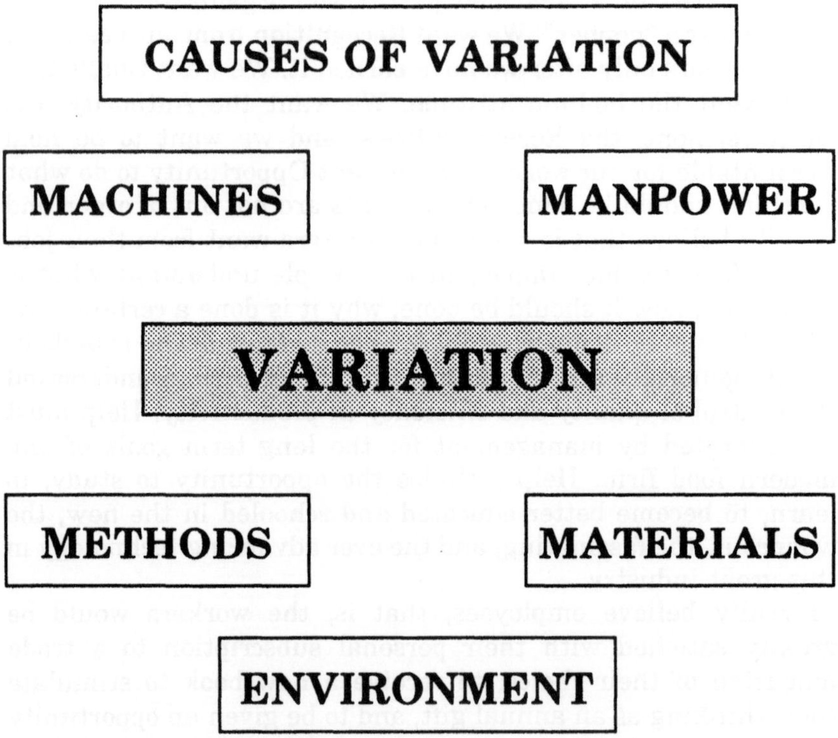

Taken From - Wilbur A. Gould
TOTAL QUALITY MANAGEMENT
FOR THE FOOD INDUSTRIES

CHAPTER 4

DIFFERENCES IN PEOPLE

"People need responsibility. They resist assuming it, but they cannot get along without it". John Steinbeck

People Differences

You and I are different. We may be of different sex. We may be different in our skin color. We may be different in our religion. We may be different in our genetic make-up. We may be different in our likes and dislikes. We may be different in our ages. We may be different in our temperament? We may be different in our educational background, etc.

Differences in people are important, at least, to most individuals. Differences in people, if known can be helpful in explaining why we do not always understand, why we do not always comprehend, why we do not always respond, and/or why we do not always do what is expected.

I sat in on a seminar recently conducted by Dr. Jody Potts of Dallas, Texas. She illustrated most clearly some of the differences between individuals in her discussion of Left and Right Brain dominance's. This seminar is best summarized as shown in Figure 4.1.

Brain Dominance

If one studies the brain dominance form as shown in Figure 4.1 and checks off the Left or Right side they can discern if they are Left brain dominant or Right brain dominant. If you find a fairly even number of checks in each column, then you are neither left or right brain dominant. The important point in using this information is that workers or people can be classified into groups based on this chart. It should help to explain why some people resist technical work while others enjoy the arts or the humorous side to life etc.

As Dr. Potts stated you can find the hidden power in your firm by knowing your people. She states that if you perceive information through both sides of your brain--the logical left side of your brain and the creative right side of your brain-- you can learn things twice as fast and always get the complete picture. You can learn to communicate better with employees or your peers or your competition.

She gives a simple exam as shown in Figure 4.2. If you see 16 or 17 squares you are left brain dominant, but if you see as many as 30 squares you are right brain dominant. She states that when using the powerful right brain techniques one can stay ahead of the forgetting curve and the competition because you transfer information from short to long term memory giving you instant recall. The right brain imagines things while the left brain logically analyzes and files the information for greater recall.

Dr. Potts states that thinking skills must be channeled by using both sides of the brain to perceive, remember, imagine, and make proper judgment. She concludes her seminar with exactly what this book is all about and that is using the brain power that is already in your firm. If you learn to use all the brain power available within your firm, you should improve your competitive advantage.

Temperament Types

David Kiersey in his book "Please Understand Me" describes the four temperament types of people. He classifies them as follows:

Type 1: DIONYSIAN (SP)
Type 2: EPIMETHEAN (SJ)FF
Type 3: PROMETHEAN (NT)
Type 4: APOLLONIAN (NF).

He further states that 38% of the population are either Type 1 or Type 2 while 12% of the population are Type 3 or Type 4. He uses a key word to describe each type, that is, Type 1 "Action", Type 2 "Duty", Type 3 "Power" and Type 4 "Spirit". The information in Figure 4.3 is taken from his book and it should be helpful to further describe individuals in your employ and give you a greater insight in how to work with them.

Getting Along With People

The following is taken from the "Soundings" publication as quoted from Derkin & Wise, Inc.

"There are five suggestions for getting along with people:

(1) Never miss a chance to say a kind or encouraging word to or about somebody. Praise good work no matter who does it.
(2) When you make a promise, keep it. But don't make more than you can keep.
(3) Hold your tongue. Always say less than you think. Speak softly and persuasively. How you say something often means more than what you say.
(4) Show an interest in others--in their pursuits, their work, and their families. Have fun with those who rejoice. Weep with those who mourn. Let everyone you meet, however humble, feel that you regard him or her as important.
(5) Be cheerful. Don't depress others by dwelling on your aches and pains and small disappointments. Remember, everyone has some burden to carry."

I truly believe in the following four word formula for success that applies equally well to organizations as it does to individuals: MAKE YOURSELF MORE USEFUL.

FIGURE 4.1 - Brain Dominance

LEFT SIDE OF BRAIN	RIGHT SIDE OF BRAIN
Verbal/Words	Visual/Pictures
__Sequential	__Wholeistic
__Linear	__Spatial
__Logical	__Intuitive
__Reasonable	__Emotional
__Analytical	__Creative
__Realistic	__Imaginative
__Temporal	__Timeless
__Serious	__Humorous
__Work Ethic	__Play Ethic
__Math, Science	__Art, Music

FIGURE 4.2 - How many Squares in this Figure?

FIGURE 4.3 - Temperament Types

Type 1: Dionysian (SP)–38% of population. **ACTION type**

Life is to be enjoyed through the 5 senses.
Freedom required, risk needed.
Play ethic.
Spontaneous, impulsive-lives to the present moment.
Non-judgmental, generous, fraternal.
Realistic: notices details.
Sensible, pragmatic, down-to-earth.
Troubleshooter, negotiator.
Careers: entrepreneur, performer, sales, sports.

Type 2: Epimethean (SJ) 38% of population. **DUTY type.**

Life is be lived usefully.
Methodical, orderly, organized.
Trustworthy, loyal--Rock of Gibraltar.
Tradition, authority important.
Bound, obliged.
Security needed.
Work ethic.
Judgmental; pessimistic--originated Murphy's law.
Careers: Lawyer, accountant, teacher (56% of public school teacher in U.S. are SJ Type.

Continued on page 22

FIGURE 4.3 - Temperament Types - Continued

Type 3: Promethean (NT)-12% of the Population. **POWER Type.**

Life is for growth.
Competence valued.
Knowledge hunger, open mind.
Work ethic
Visionary: builder of models and systems.
Enjoys the challenge of problem solving.
Slow to start; gathers all the facts first.
Economy of words: reserved, aloof.
Non judgmental of others, but self critical.
Careers: Professor, scientist, architect, Chairman of the Board

Type 4: Apollonian (NF) - 12% Of population. **SPIRIT type.**

Relationships central.
Nurtures growth in self and others; sees potential for good in everyone.
Integrity, responsibility important.
Freedom, independence required.
Optimistic, happy confident, fun-full of joy.
Play ethic.
Imaginative, intuitive, empathetic.
Verbal fluency; flair for the dramatic.
Non-judgmental of others, but extremely self-critical.
Catalyst: brings people together.
Careers: Media, counselor, personnel manager, PR, psychologist, teacher (36% of public school teachers).

Chapter 5

Training

There is a significant passion in the food industry to strive for customer quality in every package of food produced, processed and packaged.

Our first effort in human resource improvement has to be proper training of all of our people, particularly the new employee. The industry is getting too technical to allow people to just go do their thing without proper instruction or training. Technology has improved greatly in recent years and the new employee may not be equipped to handle the assigned task.

Some new employees may be well educated with college degrees in food processing, food science, food technology, food engineering, food production, management, marketing, quality assurance, etc. However, many new employees have not had the opportunity to attend college and many may not have even completed high school, therefore, they need much attention when brought on board. This attention may be from seminars, workshops, vocational, or even trade schools to help bring them up to speed.

The industry has accomplished much with the personnel who have been "brought up in the business" or learned from the school of "hard knocks". Regardless, times have changed and the individual firm must change with the times. Computers, electronic controls, automation, and sophistication of machines, methods, and materials have required personnel who must be able to read, comprehend, and, yes, daily study to stay abreast of the times.

Obtaining educated personnel is the ideal way to move forward. However, not every firm can afford the luxury of all college graduates or the expense of educating existing personnel. Therefore, they resort to their own method of training.

Training Defined

Training can be defined as "a shortcut alternative to learning from experience or from accumulated mistakes"
or it is a practice "to instruct so as to make proficient or qualified". There are many kinds of training to provide people skills, technical skills, and/or administrative skills. Each skill is important, but largely determined by the individual and their particular area of interest, expertise, and job responsibility.

Training is the pathway to growth.
Training builds confidence and self esteem,
that is, believe in self.
Training builds independence.

All food plant workers must first understand that quality is conformance to requirements. One rule: you cannot improve what is not understood. Therefore, you must have the right information at the right place and at the right time.

Growth Of A Firm

The growth of a food company is based on the growth of its people. Many food firms today allocate form 2 to 5% of their annual operating budget for actual training of their personnel. This may not be enough; but, at least, it is a start and it is in the right direction for improvement to provide a work force that can cope with the changes that are forthcoming.

Objectives Of Training

The objectives of training are to support the needs of the food firm, to teach new skills, and to convey new knowledge.

How To Train People

There are many ways to train people, the following are some examples:

1. On the job, that is, one on one, sometimes called the big brother approach. There are problems with the big brother approach in that big brother may not be a good teacher. Secondly, big brother may force a new worker to produce without being ready. Thirdly, big brother may leave out or not fully explain all that the new hire should know. (The big brother may not always see the trees from the forest). And fourthly, the trainee or new hire learns only the particular task, that is, he or she does not see the big picture.

2. A second and better method is allowing the new hire to attend formal classes at a recognized educational center or institution, such as, high school (if the new hire has not completed), a vocational or trade school, and colleges or universities (depending on previous level of education of new hire). This education should be directed and the new hire should indicate his or her intentions upon completing course or studies.

3. Another method of bringing new hires up to speed is to provide them with videos, tapes, texts and manuals to study at home and to conduct in-house seminars or send their personnel to sponsored workshops or seminars. Many workers today have access to VCR's, thus, take home videos etc. are not out of order if the new hire is truly interested in a future with your firm. I firmly believe that the new hire should have a workbook that he or she must complete in a given time and they should be checked for their retained knowledge.

A practice that has been going on since the early 70's for the low acid food processor is the FDA "Better Process Control Schools". This program has given selected employees a good understanding of some of the basic fundamentals of food processing and why it is most essential to be certain of the current process and the integrity of the container. However, this program does not go far enough as to how to really improve the process, the product, or the tools for significant control of the process and product quality. In most cases this is left up to the individual. Hopefully, they can accomplish their goal and help the firm to continue to grow.

My hope would be that today's food industry would adopt one of the above practices or alternatives to them for bringing their personnel up to a given level of education. We must remember that these people are preparing, processing, and preserving food for you and I to eat. They do the best they can with what knowledge they have. Many personnel in the food industry who I work with seek new information and they want to always do right. They want to be sure that the food they have responsibility for is not contaminated and that it is safe, wholesome, and nutritious. I am sure that is what the industry wants, but incidences in recent years would indicate that there are problems in being able to achieve this goal. So, training and retraining is most important and much needed to stay up, at least, to meet the competition.

Professional Organizations

I should add that another great training tool is through the professional organizations that are available to most personnel in the food industry. State, area, and national food processing associations exist and many offer well organized workshops, seminars, and conferences for the benefit of the industry.

The Institute of Food Technologists (IFT) has regional sections around the US and the World for help to some 27,000 professional food technologists. This organization holds an annual meeting where papers and posters, and educational displays are most helpful and informative. In addition, IFT publishes at least two journals that carry articles from a very scientific standpoint to technical production matters.

The American Society of Quality Control (ASQC) likewise publishes several journals and conducts annual meetings and monthly meetings in most major cities of USA. This organization may even offer tours of facilities wherein quality improvement programs are discussed and demonstrated.

Then, there are many commodity organizations or state, national and World wide in membership. Such organizations as

The American Society for Horticultural Science (ASHS) and the *Potato Association of America* (PAA) are examples.

I would be remiss if I did not mention *The National Food Processors Association* (NFPA). They are one of the other truly helpful educational groups in this industry. They produce many scientific/technical bulletins, flyers, and publications.

I also wish to applaud the individual suppliers who provide 'face to face' visits with the processors. I have found this segment of the food industry most knowledgeable in their sphere of activity. They are most helpful in providing new information and explaining the benefits to the individual food firm.

Subscription To Publications

Lastly, there are many trade publications which are informative, helpful, and most constructive in providing information to keep one reasonably tuned in to the new developments. Many of these publications are vertical in nature while others cut across the food industry and provide generic facts that are most useful.

I am a member or I subscribe to over 20 organizations or publications and I find great satisfaction in knowing what is being published is a contribution to this great industry for the benefit of mankind.

Advantages Of Training

There are many advantages to training personnel:

1. The worker will feel secure about new job.

2. Barriers between old and new workers are broken down.

3. Workers develop a sense of pride in their work because they are now wanted by their firm.

4. Stress levels are decreased.

5. Quality is improved.

6. With proper training, process capabilities are known.

Costs Of Not Training

There are, also, many obvious costs of not training personnel within any given food operation. Some of these are:

1. Re-work or out of specification products.
2. Dissatisfaction or complaints from the customer.
3. Loss of market share due to inferior product(s).
4. Overtime costs within the operation.
5. Underutilization of facilities and human resources.
6. Increased inspection costs
7. Absenteeism
8. Drug related sicknesses.
9. Excessive personnel turnover.
10. Willful sabotage.
11. Resistance to change and progress by personnel.
12. Apathy, low moral, no pride in work.
13. Accidents
14. Downtime
15. Avoidable mistakes.
16. No generation of quality culture.
17. Recall of products from the marketing channels.

In this day, a firm must take the proper time and provide the necessary resources to train their personnel.

Even the most sophisticated individual can learn much from his or her peers and "training" for them may be only through conversation on a neutral ground. They need this "training" the same as the new "hire" and they must constantly get refresher courses at their level to stay up-to-date. Some firms are very good at keeping their personnel up-to-date while others are most lax. Growth in the food firm today is going to happen to those firms that have personnel who are leading the industry.

CHAPTER 6

HUMAN RESOURCES AUDIT

This Chapter prepared by

STEVEN B. WHEELER
Human Resource Consultant
Wheeler & Associates
Phoenix, MD 21131

This general outline will assist you to determine those areas that should be audited by your organization.

Before starting an audit one needs to understand the commitments to time, money and support required.

The necessity of the support of top management is essential, both resources needed to complete the audit and the determination to follow through and make necessary changes.

The organizations effort should be toward ensuring that if there is a need to comply what it is and if there's not a need then remove the information or establish a "retention" policy.

Other assistance in conducting this audit can be found within your own organization or can be obtained through the use of external consultants. Also you should look to your industry groups and associations. Local, State and Federal Governments can also provide information and advice, but we need to understand how to use these resources and use them with discretion.

Other specialists that you may want to include but not limited to:

- Legal Counsel
- Medical Specialists
- Safety Professionals
- Risk Management/Workers Compensation Professionals
- Insurance Specialists
- Employee Benefits Professionals
- Educators/Trainers and Other Reliable Sources
- Human Resource Consultant(s)

The following pages list many areas that can, and have, generated governmental investigation and/or litigation and private litigation. The list should be viewed as an "issue spotting" tool- its purpose is to provide an illustration of how broad an audit can be and to suggest areas an employer might want to pursue.

A. Hiring

1. Application forms
    a. Equal Employment Opportunity Law (EEO)
    b. Americans with Disabilities Act (ADA)
    c. State Requirements (Lie Detector Statements)
    d. Desired statements (e.g., effect of providing false information)
    e. Authorization to check sources with release
    f. Credit check requirements
    g. Expiration
    h. Record retention requirements
    i. Affirmative action statistics (gov't contractors) sex, race and ethnic group identification.
    j. Applicant Flow Log
    k. I-9 Form (Immigration Reform Control Act)
    l. Contractual Disclaimer
    m. Applicant Acknowledgement

2. Recruiting Efforts
    a. Non-discriminatory advertisements
    b. Sources

c. Affirmative Action (gov't contractors)
d. Drug Free Workplace
e. Smoke Free Workplace

3. Evaluation Process
   a. ADA accommodation/hiring process
   b. Non-discriminatory criteria
   c. Validation of testing
   d. Interview structure, training
   e. Reference checks
   f. Resume verification
   g. Pre-employment physical (ADA)
   h. Drug/Alcohol testing (required/options)

4. Documentation
   a. Basis for decision/Applicant Referral
   b. Centralization
   c. Record retention requirements
   d. Statistics

5. Decision Making
   a. Training for decision makers

B. Advancement
   1. Employee indication of interest
   2. Training opportunities

C. Personnel Files
   1. Standardization of contents
   2. I-9 Forms (separate from personal and medical files)
   3. Separation of medical records
   4. Confidentiality
   5. Employee access
   6. Separate D.O.T. Files

D. Drug/Alcohol Testing
   1. ADA issues, particularly alcohol
   2. Required testing for regulated industries (D.O.T., D.O.D., F.A.A., etc.)

3. Drug-Free Workplace policies
4. State/local regulations
5. Privacy issues
6. Accurate, reliable procedures
    a. Qualified laboratory (National Institute Drug Abuse Certified)
    b. Sample collection
    c. Chain of custody
    d. Confirmation
    e. Applicant/Employee Notification
    f. Medical review officer
    g. Retest
7. Releases/Consent forms
8. Confidentiality
9. Supervisory training

E. Handbooks, Contracts, Policies
1. Consistency
2. Legality
3. Disclaimers
4. Congruence between handbook/rules/contracts and practice
5. Update as law changes
6. Distribution/Receipts
7. Identification of problem areas

F. Security
1. Non-Competition Agreements
2. Non-Disclosure Agreements
3. Search procedures/Practices
4. Surveillance Procedures/Practices
5. Electronic Monitoring
6. Negligent Retention
7. Employee Security/Safety
8. Lie Detector Procedures

G. Wages
1. Record Making/Recordkeeping
   a. Time records
   b. Payroll records
   c. Collective bargaining agreements, contracts creating wage arrangements
   d. Training wage
   e. Notice posting
2. Minimum Wage
   a. State of local law
   b. Training wage requirements
   c. Deductions
   d. Reporting, call-In, on-call
   e. Training
3. Overtime Work
   a. Record of hours worked
   b. Salaried employees
   c. Exempt employees
   d. State or local law
   e. Time not worked
   f. Scheduling, notice
   g. Required overtime
   h. Incentive pay
   i. "Comp" time

4. Equal Pay/Non-Discrimination Issues
   a. Segregated job categories
   b. Pay differentials for women, minorities
   c. Documentation for basis for differentials

5. Required Deductions/Withholding
   a. Federal, state and local income tax withholding and forms
   b. Unemployment taxes
   c. FICA
   d. Independent contractors
   e. Leased/temporary employees

6. Other Deductions
    a. State or local law
    b. Policies authorizing deductions
    c. Authorization forms

7. Employee Appraisals
    a. Defined criteria
    b. Consistency
    c. Documentation
    d. Minimize subjectivity
    e. Record retention requirements

H. Fringe Benefits

1. Vacations, Holidays, Personal Leave, Sick Leave, Other Leaves
    a. Accurate and complete description
    b. Qualification
    c. Accumulation/vesting
    d. Scheduling/work on holiday
    e. Conditions
    f. Forfeiture of pay
    g. Carry-over
    h. Level of compensation
    i. Mandated leave

2. Leaves of Absence/Disability
    a. Clear description
    b. Compliance with 1993 Family and Medical Leave Act
    c. Non-Discrimination
    d. Interaction with paid leave, worker's compensation
    e. Treatment of benefits
    f. Veteran's, Reservists Rights

3. Insurance Benefits
    a. Clear description
    b. Consistency of all descriptions
    c. Qualification

d. Flexibility to alter or eliminate program
e. ERISA compliance
f. COBRA compliance
g. Compliance with state and local law
h. Competent administration
i. Minimization of employer liability
j. Employee obligations (e.g. co-pay)
k. Coordination of benefits
l. Clear definition of when benefits terminate (Family and Medical Leave Act Compliance)
m. Multi-employer plans

4. Pension Benefits & Deferred Compensation
   a. Qualified v.Non-Qualified
   b. Tax consequences
   c. ERISA compliance
   d. Multi-employer plans
   e. Area for expert consultation only

I. Discipline and Discharge
   1. Rules
      a. Accomplishment of company goals
      b. Distribution
      c. Penalties
   2. Progressive Discipline
      a. Written notice
      b. Acknowledgement by employee
      c. Copies to employee
      d. Consistency
   3. Decision Making
      a. Oversight
      b. Suspension pending investigation
      c. Non-discrimination
      d. Fairness
      e. Contractual restraints
   4. Appeal Procedure
      a. Procedures e.g. Open Door/Grievance System
      b. Credibility
      c. Usefulness as tool

d. Final authority
e. Binding effect

5. Documentation
    a. Recordkeeping requirements
    b. Disciplinary record
    c. Statements, relevant records
    d. Documentation of basis for decision
    e. Written notices to employee with basis
6. Exit procedures
    a. Return of keys, company property
    b. Affirmative of non-disclosure, non-compete agreements
    c. Exit interview
    d. References
7. Compliance with WARN (Worker Adjustment Retraining Notification)

J. Communications
1. Handbooks, Policies
2. Employee Committees, <u>Electromation</u> Issues
3. Union Avoidance
    a. Solicitation/Distribution
    b. Concerted activity
    c. Prior union activity
    d. Employee dissatisfaction level
    e. Signs of organizing
4. Complaint Resolution Procedures
    a. Encourage dispute resolution in-house
    b. Specification of procedure
    c. Effectiveness
    d. Tracking trends
    e. Credibility
    f. Appropriate level of confidentiality

K. Safety
1. OSHA compliance
    a. General duty clause
    b. Industry/practice specific regulations
    c. Logs
    d. Reports illness or injury

            e. Exposure/medical records
            f. Hazardous substance regulations
            g. Industry/practice specific recordkeeping requirements
            h. State or local variations
            i. Procedures for dealing with government investigation
            j. Notice posting
        2. Transportation Operations
            a. DOT coverage
            b. Driver qualification
            c. Driver safety
            d. Logs/recordkeeping requirements
            e. Equipment safety
            f. Surface Transportation Assistance Act
            g. Drug/alcohol testing
        3. Safety program
            a. Safety rules
            b. Training
            c. Meetings
            d. Inspections
            e. Reporting unsafe conditions
            f. Accident investigation
            g. Drug testing
            h. Remedy of unsafe conditions
            i. Discipline for safety violations
            j. Record-making and recordkeeping
L. Supervision
    1. Authority/Responsibility
    2. Training
        a. Policies, procedures, rules
        b. Equal employment opportunity
        c. Americans with Disabilities Act
        d. Employment torts (privacy, defamation, wrongful discharge)
        e. Documentation
        f. Performance appraisals
        g. Sexual harassment
        h. Issues of particular concern to employer

3. Lines of Communication
    a. Encouragement of consultation on questionable issues
    b. Supervisor feedback

M. Equal Employment Opportunity
1. Administrative
    a. EEO-1 Form
    b. Recordkeeping requirements
    c. Notice posting
    d. Procedures for dealing with investigations
2. Harassment
    a. Sexual harassment policy and procedure
    b. Policy prohibiting harassment on other basis
    c. Assessment of working atmosphere
    d. Employee/supervisory training
3. Assessment of Potential Problem Areas
    a. Segregated classifications
    b. Consistency of treatment
    c. Pay differentials
    d. Actual or perceived barriers to advancement
    e. Age issues, national origin issues, religion issues
    f. Disparate impact/business necessity
4. ADA Compliance
    a. Procedures
    b. Training
    c. Barrier Elimination
    d. Public Accommodation Issues
    e. Work Accommodation
    f. Union involvement

N. State and local laws affecting employment

Many states and local jurisdictions have laws that regulate the employment relationship. State and local laws may be more protective of employees than federal law (for example, in the discrimination area, cover more types of discrimination than federal law). Areas often covered by state or local law include:

1. Additional bases for prohibited discrimination (e.g., sexual orientation, marital status, personal appearance).
2. Workplace safety
3. Drug testing
4. Plant closings and layoffs
5. Smoking
6. Workers Compensation
7. Public policies
8. Wrongful discharge
9. Lie detector tests

Required Employment Posters;

Federal -

Equal Employment Opportunity
Family Medical Leave Act 1993
Minimum Wage
Americans with Disabilities Act
Employee Polygraph
Occupational Safety Health

State - (Various depending on your State Requirements e.g.)

Unemployment,
Human Rights,
Workers Compensation,
Minimum Wage, etc.

Local - Check with your local government to determine if there are postings required.

CHAPTER 7

THE NEW EMPLOYEE

This Chapter prepared in cooperation with

STEVEN B. WHEELER
Human Resource Consultant
Wheeler & Associates
Phoenix, MD 21131

Give a person a fish and he can eat for a day,
but teach a person how to fish and he can eat for a lifetime.
Anon.

Application Form

This application form can be used for both General and D.O.T. (pre-employment) situations. It covers Equal Employment, Americans with Disabilities Act, and appropriate release concerning substance abuse testing, references, and employment "at will". Also included, is an "Applicant Acknowledgement Form" for applicants to indicate their understanding of the job duties. If the employer has a contract with the federal government, they should consider the development of a "Post-Application for Employment". This form can collect required information regarding:

- Sex
- Ethnic Group

- Vietnam War-Veteran
- Disability Status - for reasonable accommodation

Evaluation Process

Interview Procedures - These are situations where it is helpful to require a "personal requisition" and an "applicant referral" form , for tracking as to who was interviewed and the results to fulfill that vacancy. These procedures can assist to ensure non-discriminatory practices in hiring, plus document the hiring process.

Appropriate training should be given to anyone who conducts an interview as to what can and cannot be asked in the selection process. Reference checks should be done on the final applicant(s) prior to the final hiring decision making process.

Any organization which is requiring drug testing should post and advise applicants of this policy - in help wanted advertising, prior to beginning the selection process, and during the interview.

Under Americans with Disabilities Act (ADA) employers who conduct pre-employment physicals can continue this procedure only if they make such an offer "conditional" based on successfully completing a physical. They cannot use the physical to eliminate those with a disability. Also, you can no longer ask questions regarding the applicants health, medical history or previous Workers Compensation claims, etc.

Substance Abuse Testing

Familiarity with the four types of testing programs and the types of tests employed is essential to an understanding of the legal and practical issues surrounding drug and alcohol testing.

A. Testing Programs

1 **Pre-hire testing** is one of the most common types of testing. Typically, the applicant is asked to report for testing immediately after an interview. The key component of pre-hire testing is a very short interval between the request for testing and the test -- a period of a day or more may permit a drug or alcohol abuser to escape detection.

2. **Post-accident testing** programs trigger testing upon the employee's involvement in a workplace accident or mishap. The key concept is defining the circumstances that require testing. Choices include any accident, accidents that cause property damage over a certain threshold, accidents that cause personal injury or injuries that require medical attention in excess of first aid.
3. **Random testing** programs employ a random procedure (from sophisticated computer programs to picking names out of a hat) to select employees who will be tested. Selection dates can be established in advance or can be randomly selected.
4. **Reasonable suspicion testing** may be part of a formal testing program or may simply occur in the absence of a testing program because an employee's behavior gives rise to a "reasonable suspicion" of drug or alcohol use. Reasonable suspicion testing should not be implemented without training supervisors how to recognize signs of alcohol and/or drug use and how to correctly approach employees to require testing.

B. **Testing Procedures**

1. **Alcohol tests** can be performed via breathalyzer, urine or blood testing. The perferred testing protocol is performance of a breathalyzer test, if that test is positive, the collection of a blood sample for laboratory testing. Only breathalyzer and blood tests have been recognized as accurate measures of alcohol impairment; urine testing is less reliable. Where an employer seeks an alcohol test, it should request that breathalyzer and/or blood testing be performed. Some collection facilities simply collect a urine sample unless a specific request is made.
2. **Drug tests** are typically performed on urine samples. The initial test performed is a "screening" test, so-called because the accuracy level of the test is typically not high, but it is an inexpensive means of "screening out" negative samples that do not warrant more sophisticated, more accurate and more expensive confirmatory tests.

Federal guidelines and some state laws require employers to have confirmatory test performed. These tests are performed on the same urine sample, and a portion of the sample is preserved to permit a later retest, if requested or necessary. The most common confirmatory test is the gas chromatography/mass spectrometry (GC/MS). CG/MS confirmation, when performed by a qualified laboratory, is virtually 100% accurate. Drug tests, however, unlike alcohol tests, often do not measure impairment. They test for the presence of certain by-products of drug use in the urine. They indicate use of a drug with a period that varies from 24 hours to 30 days, depending upon the drug.

3. **New Technologies:** Increased interest in testing has spurred the development of more accurate and less invasive testing methods. Methods being evaluated include hair analysis, ocular response tests that evaluate eye movement and pupil reactions, and electronic simulators that measure hand-eye coordination, motor control and mental alertness. Proponents of hair testing assert that it can be used to detect drug use of 30 days or more. Collection of hair samples is less invasive than urine or blood tests. The accuracy of hair testing is still being debated. Groups that object to employers taking action based upon off-duty behavior rather than impairment object to hair testing because it simply measures historic use.

Ocular testing detects eye and pupil reactions associated with use of alcohol or particular drugs. It is expected to be used in conjunction with existing alcohol and drug testing to confirm use.

Electronic testing does not detect drug or alcohol use, but simply measures whether the employee's coordination, motor control or alertness has deteriorated, compared against baseline scores. The technology is being tested in the transportation, petroleum and distribution industry.

Drug/Alcohol Testing: Drug Free Workplace Policies

The Drug Free Workplace Act of 1988 requires businesses that are parties to a federal government contract which provides goods and services in the amount of $25,000 or more to certify that they provide a drug free workplace for employees directly engaged in the performance of work. To comply with the Act the contractor must:

- Notify employees in writing and post a notice that any employee who unlawfully manufactures, sells, or uses or has in their possession a prohibited controlled substance will be subject to sanctions.
- Develop an education and awareness program.
- Provide each employee with a copy of the drug free policy.
- Advise employees they must report to their employer within 5 days of the occurrence a drug conviction or drug workplace conviction.
- Inform the federal agency within 10 days of receiving a notice of an employee's conviction.
- Make a "good faith" effort to maintain a drug free workplace.
- Take necessary disciplinary action of the convicted employee to discipline, discharge or rehabilitate by an approved agency.

The Act does not require that federal contractors implement a drug testing program or establish a drug rehabilitation program.

Wages: Record Making/Keeping

Most employers develop and maintain effective record keeping of who works, what hours and at what rate of pay.

However, a common violation of these basic elements can result in an assessment of substantial back pay.

Employers are well advised to have all employees either punch a time clock or record on a time sheet hours worked, holidays, vacation, sickness, etc. These time sheets should be completed by the employee themselves showing lunch breaks, work breaks, start and stop work time and other approved absences.

An area that surfaces frequently is when employers are held accountable for time worked even if it's not recorded, i.e. when an employee comes to work early or stays late with or without your approval are entitled to be compensated.

Time records should be retained for up to a three year period.

The Wage-Hour division requires all employers to post notices that generally explain the provisions of the Act.

Lastly, most investigations are conducted as a result of complaints from employees who have been fired or feel that they have been mistreated.

Once an investigation begins it can be enlarged to other aspects, like former employees, as well as current employees. Also, who is exempt and non-exempt, are they being compensated at the appropriate level according to the Act.

Handbook

The human resources officer should provide the employee with a written hand book of the above. Ideally, the above should be presented orally, visually (Video), and in writing to each employee. The latter should be in a 3-ring notebook so that the handbook can be kept current.

Of major importance, the specific position the applicant is filing for should be described and defined in detail and the applicant should have their job responsibilities clearly defined and set-forth in writing.

Agreement

After the interview and the applicant has been accepted, he/she will comply with requirements as set-forth during the interview, and that he/she will support the Mission and Vision Statements to the best of their ability as stated by management.

Progress Evaluation

At the end of the first day, end of the first week, and at the end of the first month the progress of the new employee should be discussed with him by his or her superiors and the human resource manager. Of prime importance is detailing the new employees strong and weak points with sufficient explanation as to where they do presently stand with the employer and an indication of their future with the firm. If the employee is lacking in proper training for the position he/she must be willing to attend classes as designated by the firm to assist the individual in pursuit of the job. The firm must be willing to set aside time and resources to permit any needed training programs. The employee must remove the fear of loss of his job and he/she must want to listen, observe, and study to learn.

Supervisory personnel and team members should always show a genuine interest in each team member and any new employee and they should always be alert to give service to the new employee. Supervisors and team leaders should never give orders, but requests and suggestions for improvement. If the new employee is not able to comply, he should resign or ask to be reassigned to other areas. Hangers-on cost firms much money and may result in many defective products, loss of production, rework, etc.

The Interview

During the first on site interview, the evaluation form as shown in Figure 7.2 should be completed. In addition the following questions should be answered by the interviewer:

FIGURE 7.1 - Interview Questions and Observations

Does the applicant appear to have the ability to adjust to the job?

YES ____ NO ____ COMMENTS: ____________________

Will the applicant be accepted by coworkers and supervisors?

YES ____ NO ____ COMMENTS: ____________________

Does the applicant have ability to do the required work?

YES ___ NO ___ COMMENTS: ____________________

Does the applicant have an interest in the job opening?

YES ___ NO ___ EXPLAIN: ____________________

Continued Over

FIGURE 7.1 - Interview Questions and Observations - Continued

Is there a possibility of the applicant remaining with our firm for a given time?

YES ___ NO ___ EXPLAIN ________________

Does the applicant show potential for growth?

YES ___ NO ___ EXPLAIN: ________________

Are there any recognizable interfering factors?

YES ___ NO ___ LIST THE FACTORS:

____

NARRATIVE COMMENTS FOLLOWING THE INTERVIEW:

____

____

Orientation

One of the first requirements in any training program for the new employee is information about the firm. Sharing this information up front will make the employee feel welcome and wanted and help him or her quickly become a part of the firm. This should be a major part of the orientation.

The orientation should, also, include the following:

__ History of the firm including the mission, vision, and value statements
__ Introduction of officers and key personnel
__ Relationship of firm to industry
__ Product(s) firm manufactures
__ Processing procedures

__ Location of bulletin boards and other sources of information
__ Location of job manuals, material safety data sheets (msds) book, master forms
__ Wearing of badge and use of passes, if necessary
__ Exact hours of work
__ When, Where, and How to Punch In and Punch Out
__ Lunch periods, breaks, location of lunch area
__ Dress code and safety factors
__ Lockers and personal property
__ Washrooms and wash up policy
__ No-smoking, gum chewing, eating policies
__ Safety equipment, rules and regulations
__ Removal of any packages from property
__ Telephone usage, personal messages
__ Lateness reporting, absenteeism
__ Housekeeping procedures
__ Human relations office-benefits, records, payroll.

FIGURE 7.2 - Interview Evaluation Example

RATING SCALE:
1 = Outstanding, 2 = Above Average,
3 = Average, 4 = Acceptable,
5 = Limited Potential

NAME ____________________

APPEARANCE: Grooming: ____
Posture: ____
Dress: ____
Manners: ____
Neatness: ____

Comments: ____________________

PREPARATION FOR INTERVIEW:
Knowledge of Firm: ____
Knowledge of Position: ____
Pertinent and Relevant Questions: ____

FIGURE 7.2 - Interview Evaluation Example - Continued

EXPRESSION: Organization: ____ Presentation: ____
Ideas: ____ Delivery:____

GOALS: Defined: ____ Realistic:____
Practical:____ Confident:____

MATURITY: Self reliant: ____ Decision Maker: ____
Responsible: ____ Shows Leadership Abilities: ____

SINCERITY: Honest: ____ Genuine: ____
Real: ____ Attitude: ____

PERSONALITY: Enthusiastic: ____ Motivated: ____
Likeable: ____ Industrious: ____
Will fit: ____ Total Individual:____

QUALIFICATIONS:
Academic Preparation: ____ Work Experience ____
Fits Position Available:____

OVERALL EDUCATION:
Long range potential: ____ Ability:____
Ambition: ____ Stability:____

CANDID COMMENTS:
Strong Points: ____

____

Weak Notes: ____

____

Suggestions: ____

____

Other: ____

____

Interviewer: ______________________________ Date: ________

FIGURE 7.3 - Remember This

IF YOU WORK FOR A MAN, in Heaven's name WORK for him....If he pays you wages which supply you bread and butter, WORK for him; speak well of him; stand by him and stand by the firm he represents....If put to a pinch, an ounce of loyalty is worth a pound of cleverness....If you must vilify, condemn and eternally disparage---resign your position, and when you are outside, damn to your heart's content, but as long as you are part of the firm do not condemn it....If you do that, you are loosening the tendrils that are holding you to the firm, and at the first high wind that comes along, you will be uprooted and blown away, and probably will never know the reason why.

ELBERT HUBBARD

FIGURE 7.4 - Cost Of Absenteeism
(Taken from Commerce Clearing House)

A. Sick hours cost mid-sized companies 2.21% of all paid productive hours amounting to some $411.00 per year for each worker on unscheduled absences.

B. In smaller companies (<than 500 employees), it cost them almost $457.00 PER YEAR.

C. In addition to Wages and Salary, hidden costs include the following:

1. Overtime to cover costs for the persons absence,

2. Temporary help to fill in for absent person,

3. Supervisors' time spent in rearranging work schedules,

4. Decreased moral and lower productivity among people who have to work harder to cover for someone who creates an absentee problem,

5. Catch up time for someone returning from an absence, and

6. Lost income and customer dissatisfaction when service quality goes down because of understaffing caused by absences.

WAGCO

123 Main Street, Columbus, KL 99511
AN EQUAL OPPORTUNITY EMPLOYER

Pre-Employment Application

Please Print Answer every question fully and accurately

Date____________ Social Security Number __________ - __________ - __________

Name ____
Last First Middle

Present Address ____
Number Street Apt. #

____
City State Zip Code

Telephone # ( ) ______________________, OR ( ) ____________________

Position Desired __________________________________ Date Available _______

Minimum Wage/Salary Expected ______________________________________

Applying For: _______ Full Time, _______ Temporary, _______ Part Time

Are you 18 years of age or older? Yes _______________ No _____________

Will you work overtime? Yes ____ No ____, Shift Work? Yes ____ No ____

How did you hear about WAGCO? ______________________________________

Have you previously work for WAGCO? Yes ____ No ____

Are you related to any employees of WAGCO? Yes ____ No ____

If yes, to whom ______________________________ Relationship __________

Are you now Employed? Yes ____ No ____

If yes, may we inquire of your present employer? Yes ____ No ____
If no, please explain. ______________________________________
If you have been <u>convicted</u> of a felony in the last 5 years, on what charges?

When? ___________________ Describe _____________________________
(NOTE: Prior conviction information is not necessarily a bar to consideration of employment)

EMPLOYMENT HISTORY

List the names of your previous employers in chronological order with present or last employer listed first, including any period of unemployment. If self-employed, give firm name.

Present or last employer ____________________ Address __________________

Start date __________ Departure date __________ Starting pay ___________

Final pay __________ Reason for leaving ________________________________

Job Title ________________Name of Supervisor & Title ___________________

Description of work and responsibilities _________________________________

____

____

Next previous employer ____________________ Address __________________

Start date __________ Departure date __________ Starting pay ___________

Final pay __________ Reason for leaving ________________________________

Job Title ________________Name of Supervisor & Title ___________________

Description of work and responsibilities _________________________________

____

____

Next previous employer ____________________ Address __________________

Start date __________ Departure date __________ Starting pay ___________

Final pay __________ Reason for leaving ________________________________

Job Title ________________Name of Supervisor & Title ___________________

Description of work and responsibilities _________________________________

____

____

DRIVING HISTORY

ONLY IF APPLYING FOR A DRIVING POSITION COMPLETE THIS PAGE.
A VALID COPY OF YOUR CURRENT DRIVING RECORD IS REQUIRED AT THE TIME OF COMPLETION AND/OR SUBMISSION OF THIS INFORMATION .

Address for past three years ______________________________
Number Street Apt. #

____
City State ZIP Code
(Attach sheet if more space is needed)

List all driver licenses currently held.

State	License(s) No.	Type	Expiration Date

A. Have you ever been disqualified or denied a license, permit or privilge to operate a moter vehicle by a federal, state or local goverment?
Yes ____ No ____

B. Has any license, permit or privilege ever been suspended or revoked, by a federal, state or local goverment?
Yes ____ No ____

C. Advise if license(s) or privilege has been reinstated or requalified.
Yes ____ No ____

D. Have you ever been disqualified under Federal Dept. of Transportation Driver Qualification or Regulations?
Yes ____ No _____

If the answer to either A, B or D is Yes, Attach statement giving details, including reasons and dates.

Driving History (Continued)

Class of Equipment	Type of Eqipment (Van, Tank, Flat,)	Dates From	Dates To
Straight Truck			
Tractor and Semi-Trailer			
Tractor-Two-Trailer			

List states operated in for last five years ______________________________

____

Indicate special courses or training successfully completed

____

Safe Driving awards recieved and from whom? ______________________

ACCIDENT RECORD FOR PAST 3 YEARS. List dates and details of any accident in which you have been involved as the operater of a motor vehicle, specifying date and nature of each accident and any fatalities or personal injury it caused. (Attach sheet if more space is needed)

____

____

____

____

____

____

TRAFFIC CONVICTIONS AND FOREFITURES for the past 3 years (other than parking violations). List types of violations and date.

Attach sheet if more space is needed.

____

____

EDUCATIONAL HISTORY

Last school attended Name and Address	Last Year Completed (circle one)	Did you Graduate? Yes or No
High School	1 2 3 4	
Technical School	1 2 3 4	
College	1 2 3 4	

List any special experience, qualifications or skills, that you believe would help you do the job for which you applied.
Typing - W.P.M. __________ or other Office Equipment, Word Processor, Computer, etc. (Be specific)

____

____

____

____

Mechnical, welding or types of equipment operated, etc. and permits or certificates held or recieved, i.e., Certified Welder. (Be specific)

____

____

____

____

"READ THE FOLLOWING CONDITIONS CAREFULLY AND SIGN TO INDICATE YOUR AGREEMENT"

I hereby certify that the information on this application is accurate. I understand that any false answers or statements or misrepresentations by omission, made by me on the application or any related document, will be sufficient for rejection of my application or for my immediate discharge should such falsifications or misrepresentations be discovered at any time after I am employed.

I hereby agree that, if so requested by the Company, and at no personal expense, I will undergo a physical examination to determine whether I am physically qualified to perform my assigned job, and I agree that the physician may disclose to the Company results of such examination. If hired, I agree to undergo physical examinations as may be requested by the Company as a requirement of my continued employment. I understand that all physical examinations may include drug and alcohol testing, and that successful completion of these examinations will be a condition of employment or continued employment.

This application will be considered only if you have specified the particular position for which you are applying and will be considered to be active for thirty (30) days. If you wish to be considered for employment after that time, you must reapply.

This application does not constitute an express or implied contract of employment. If an employment relationship is established, I understand that both I and the Company have the right to terminate the employment relationship at any time, with or without cause. I understand that, if hired, I will be an at- will employee and that this at-will employment status can only be altered by an express written agreement signed by myself, and an officer of the Company.

I attest that the information provided herein is true and complete to the best of my knowledge. I hereby knowingly and voluntarily authorize the Company to investigate my past record as may be necessary and I release my employers and all persons whomsoever from any and all liability from damage on account of furnishing said information.

Signature of Applicant ______________________________

Date ________________________

WAGCO

APPLICANT ACKNOWLEDGEMENT FORM

(To be completed during interview process)

I hereby acknowledge that the duties, tasks and functions of the position for which I am applying have been fully described to me. I certify that:

___ I am able to perform the duties, tasks and functions of the position for which I am applying without any accomodation.

___ I am able to perform the duties, tasks and functions of the position for which I am applying with the following accommodation:

____

____

____

____

Date: ______________ Signature: ________________________

Print name: ________________________

Immigrant Employment Eligibility

The Immigration Reform and Control Act of 1986, which is administered by The Department of Justice, U.S. Immigration and Naturalization Service, which has offices in all states as well as Guam, Puerto Rico and The U.S. Virgin Islands, publishes a *Handbook For Employers, Instructions for Completing Form I-9.* This form booklet contains an Employment Eligibility Verification Form with Instructions.

FIGURE 7.5 - Instructions For I-9, Employment Eligibility Verification

U.S. Department of Justice
Immigration and Naturalization Service

OMB No. 1115-0136
Employment Eligibility Verification

INSTRUCTIONS

PLEASE READ ALL INSTRUCTIONS CAREFULLY BEFORE COMPLETING THIS FORM.

Anti-Discrimination Notice. It is illegal to discriminate against any individual (other than an alien not authorized to work in the U.S.) in hiring, discharging, or recruiting or referring for a fee because of that individual's national origin or citizenship status. It is illegal to discriminate against work eligible individuals. Employers **CANNOT** specify which document(s) they will accept from an employee. The refusal to hire an individual because of a future expiration date may also constitute illegal discrimination.

Section 1 - Employee. All employees, citizens and noncitizens, hired after November 6, 1986, must complete Section 1 of this form at the time of hire, which is the actual beginning of employment. **The employer is responsible for ensuring that Section 1 is timely and properly completed.**

Preparer/Translator Certification. The Preparer/Translator Certification must be completed if Section 1 is prepared by a person other than the employee. A preparer/translator may be used only when the employee is unable to complete Section 1 on his/her own. However, the employee must still sign Section 1 personally.

Section 2 - Employer. For the purpose of completing this form, the term "employer" includes those recruiters and referrers for a fee who are agricultural associations, agricultural employers, or farm labor contractors.

Employers must complete Section 2 by examining evidence of identity and employment eligibility within three (3) business days of the date employment begins. If employees are authorized to work, but are unable to present the required document(s) within three business days, they must present a receipt for the application of the document(s) within three business days and the actual document(s) within ninety (90) days. However, if employers hire individuals for a duration of less than three business days, Section 2 must be completed at the time employment begins. **Employers must record**: **1)** document title; **2)** issuing authority; **3)** document number, **4)** expiration date, if any; and **5)** the date employment begins. Employers must sign and date the certification. Employees must present original documents. Employers may, but are not required to, photocopy the document(s) presented. These photocopies may only be used for the verification process and must be retained with the I-9. **However, employers are still responsible for completing the I-9.**

Section 3 - Updating and Reverification. Employers must complete Section 3 when updating and/or reverifying the I-9. Employers must reverify employment eligibility of their employees on or before the expiration date recorded in Section 1. Employers **CANNOT** specify which document(s) they will accept from an employee.

- If an employee's name has changed at the time this form is being updated/ reverified, complete Block A.
- If an employee is rehired within three (3) years of the date this form was originally completed and the employee is still eligible to be employed on the same basis as previously indicated on this form (updating), complete Block B and the signature block.
- If an employee is rehired within three (3) years of the date this form was originally completed and the employee's work authorization has expired **or** if a current employee's work authorization is about to expire (reverification), complete Block B and:
  - examine any document that reflects that the employee is authorized to work in the U.S. (see List A **or** C),
  - record the document title, document number and expiration date (if any) in Block C, and
  - complete the signature block.

Photocopying and Retaining Form I-9. A blank I-9 may be reproduced provided both sides are copied. The Instructions must be available to all employees completing this form. Employers must retain completed I-9s for three (3) years after the date of hire **or** one (1) year after the date employment ends, whichever is later.

For more detailed information, you may refer to the INS Handbook for Employers, (Form M-274). You may obtain the handbook at your local INS office.

Privacy Act Notice. The authority for collecting this information is the Immigration Reform and Control Act of 1986, Pub. L. 99-603 (8 U.S.C. 1324a).

This information is for employers to verify the eligibility of individuals for employment to preclude the unlawful hiring, or recruiting or referring for a fee, of aliens who are not authorized to work in the United States.

This information will be used by employers as a record of their basis for determining eligibility of an employee to work in the United States. The form will be kept by the employer and made available for inspection by officials of the U.S. Immigration and Naturalization Service, the Department of Labor, and the Office of Special Counsel for Immigration Related Unfair Employment Practices.

Submission of the information required in this form is voluntary. However, an individual may not begin employment unless this form is completed since employers are subject to civil or criminal penalties if they do not comply with the Immigration Reform and Control Act of 1986.

Reporting Burden. We try to create forms and instructions that are accurate, can be easily understood, and which impose the least possible burden on you to provide us with information. Often this is difficult because some immigration laws are very complex. Accordingly, the reporting burden for this collection of information is computed as follows: **1)** learning about this form, 5 minutes; **2)** completing the form, 5 minutes; and **3)** assembling and filing (recordkeeping) the form, 5 minutes, for an average of 15 minutes per response. If you have comments regarding the accuracy of this burden estimate, or suggestions for making this form simpler, you can write to both the Immigration and Naturalization Service, 425 I Street, N.W., Room 5304, Washington, D. C. 20536; and the Office of Management and Budget, Paperwork Reduction Project, OMB No. 1115-0136, Washington, D.C. 20503.

Form I-9 (Rev. 11-21-91) N

EMPLOYERS MUST RETAIN COMPLETED I-9
PLEASE DO NOT MAIL COMPLETED I-9 TO INS

Since this information is so extensive it is recommended that you obtain a copy of the INS - Handbook For Employers for you company.

FIGURE 7.6 - I-9 Form

U.S. Department of Justice
Immigration and Naturalization Service

OMB No. 1115-0136
Employment Eligibility Verification

Please read instructions carefully before completing this form. The instructions must be available during completion of this form. ANTI-DISCRIMINATION NOTICE. It is illegal to discriminate against work eligible individuals. Employers CANNOT specify which document(s) they will accept from an employee. The refusal to hire an individual because of a future expiration date may also constitute illegal discrimination.

Section 1. Employee Information and Verification. To be completed and signed by employee at the time employment begins

Print Name: Last | First | Middle Initial | Maiden Name

Address *(Street Name and Number)* | Apt. # | Date of Birth *(month/day/year)*

City | State | Zip Code | Social Security #

I am aware that federal law provides for imprisonment and/or fines for false statements or use of false documents in connection with the completion of this form.

I attest, under penalty of perjury, that I am (check one of the following):
- ☐ A citizen or national of the United States
- ☐ A Lawful Permanent Resident (Alien # A________)
- ☐ An alien authorized to work until ___/___/___ (Alien # or Admission # ________)

Employee's Signature | Date *(month/day/year)*

Preparer and/or Translator Certification. *(To be completed and signed if Section 1 is prepared by a person other than the employee.) I attest, under penalty of perjury, that I have assisted in the completion of this form and that to the best of my knowledge the information is true and correct.*

Preparer's/Translator's Signature | Print Name

Address *(Street Name and Number, City, State, Zip Code)* | Date *(month/day/year)*

Section 2. Employer Review and Verification. To be completed and signed by employer. **Examine one document from List A OR examine one document from List B and one from List C** as listed on the reverse of this form and record the title, number and expiration date, if any, of the document(s)

	List A	**OR**	**List B**	**AND**	**List C**
Document title:	______		______		______
Issuing authority:	______		______		______
Document #:	______		______		______
Expiration Date *(if any)*:	__/__/__		__/__/__		__/__/__
Document #:	______				
Expiration Date *(if any)*:	__/__/__				

CERTIFICATION - I attest, under penalty of perjury, that I have examined the document(s) presented by the above-named employee, that the above-listed document(s) appear to be genuine and to relate to the employee named, that the employee began employment on *(month/day/year)* ___/___/___ **and that to the best of my knowledge the employee is eligible to work in the United States. (State employment agencies may omit the date the employee began employment).**

Signature of Employer or Authorized Representative | Print Name | Title

Business or Organization Name | Address *(Street Name and Number, City, State, Zip Code)* | Date *(month/day/year)*

Section 3. Updating and Reverification. To be completed and signed by employer

A. New Name *(if applicable)* | B. Date of rehire *(month/day/year) (if applicable)*

C. If employee's previous grant of work authorization has expired, provide the information below for the document that establishes current employment eligibility.

Document Title: ______ Document #: ______ Expiration Date (if any): __/__/__

I attest, under penalty of perjury, that to the best of my knowledge, this employee is eligible to work in the United States, and if the employee presented document(s), the document(s) I have examined appear to be genuine and to relate to the individual.

Signature of Employer or Authorized Representative | Date *(month/day/year)*

Form I-9 (Rev. 11-21-91) N

FIGURE 7.7 - I-9 Form, Lists of Acceptable Documents

LISTS OF ACCEPTABLE DOCUMENTS

LIST A

Documents that Establish Both Identity and Employment Eligibility

1. U.S. Passport (unexpired or expired)
2. Certificate of U.S. Citizenship *(INS Form N-560 or N-561)*
3. Certificate of Naturalization *(INS Form N-550 or N-570)*
4. Unexpired foreign passport, with *I-551 stamp or* attached *INS Form I-94* indicating unexpired employment authorization
5. Alien Registration Receipt Card with photograph *(INS Form I-151 or I-551)*
6. Unexpired Temporary Resident Card *(INS Form I-688)*
7. Unexpired Employment Authorization Card *(INS Form I-688A)*
8. Unexpired Reentry Permit *(INS Form I-327)*
9. Unexpired Refugee Travel Document *(INS Form I-571)*
10. Unexpired Employment Authorization Document issued by the INS which contains a photograph *(INS Form I-688B)*

OR

LIST B

Documents that Establish Identity

1. Driver's license or ID card issued by a state or outlying possession of the United States provided it contains a photograph or information such as name, date of birth, sex, height, eye color, and address
2. ID card issued by federal, state, or local government agencies or entities provided it contains a photograph or information such as name, date of birth, sex, height, eye color, and address
3. School ID card with a photograph
4. Voter's registration card
5. U.S. Military card or draft record
6. Military dependent's ID card
7. U.S. Coast Guard Merchant Mariner Card
8. Native American tribal document
9. Driver's license issued by a Canadian government authority

For persons under age 18 who are unable to present a document listed above:

10. School record or report card
11. Clinic, doctor, or hospital record
12. Day-care or nursery school record

AND

LIST C

Documents that Establish Employment Eligibility

1. U.S. social security card issued by the Social Security Administration *(other than a card stating it is not valid for employment)*
2. Certification of Birth Abroad issued by the Department of State *(Form FS-545 or Form DS-1350)*
3. Original or certified copy of a birth certificate issued by a state, county, municipal authority or outlying possession of the United States bearing an official seal
4. Native American tribal document
5. U.S. Citizen ID Card *(INS Form I-197)*
6. ID Card for use of Resident Citizen in the United States *(INS Form I-179)*
7. Unexpired employment authorization document issued by the INS *(other than those listed under List A)*

Illustrations of many of these documents appear in Part 8 of the Handbook for Employers (M-274)

Form I-9 (Rev. 11-21-91) N

FPI-RBK

CHAPTER 8

SEXUAL HARASSMENT

This Chapter prepared by

STEVEN B. WHEELER
Human Resource Consultant
Wheeler & Associates
Phoenix, MD 21131

Much has been written about sexual harassment, and much more will be written about this subject.

What is Sexual Harassment?
Not all sexual activity in the workplace will be defined by law as sexual harassment. To determine if there is sexual harassment in the workplace, several issues need to be examined.

- Sexual advances that are invited
- Uninvited, but welcome
- Offensive, but tolerated
- Flatly rejected

These forms of conduct can occur at the worksite, company-sponsored events, or between co-workers away from their worksite.
Generally, sexual harassment can be categorized as unacceptable Verbal, Non-Verbal, or Physical behavior. The following list serves as a guideline to determine if someone is sexually harassing you.

You are being sexually harassed if a person is:

Verbal

- Making sexual comments or innuendos to you
- Asking you about sexual fantasies, preferences or your sexual history
- Repeatedly asking you out when you have let the person know you are not interested
- Putting unwanted pressure on you for dates
- Telling you sexual jokes or stories
- Making sexual comments about your clothing, anatomy or looks
- Constantly bothering you
- Using sex as a condition for earning a promotion
- Giving you unwelcome advances
- Continuously turning work discussions into sexual jokes

Non-Verbal

- Blocking your path
- Following you
- Showing you sexual photographs or graffiti
- Staring at you
- Making sexual gestures to you using hand or body movements
- Looking you up-and-down (elevator eyes)

Physical

- Touching your clothing, hair or body
- Standing close to you or brushing up against you
- Hanging around you
- Hugging, kissing, patting or stroking you
- Touching or rubbing oneself sexually in your presence

Unwelcome activity of a sexual nature is classified as sexual harassment under the law. Sexual conduct is unwelcome when:

- acceptance or rejection of the conduct is used to make employment decisions (hiring, promotion, work assignments, pay increases) that affect the person claiming harassment;
- the conduct has the purpose or effect of unreasonable interference with the victim's job performance, or

- the conduct creates an intimidating hostile or offensive work environment.

The courts have developed a definition for several types of sexual conduct in the workplace. "Quid Pro Quo" (meaning Something for Something) harassment is the individual with the hiring/firing ability to effect an employee's working conditions and makes unwelcome sexual advances. These advances could include the employee's pay, benefits, or their refusal to submit to the demands which result in loss of pay, promotion, transfer, or in their termination!

This type of harassment can be eliminated from the workplace by proper and frequent training of supervisors and managers.

A hostile environment is the continuing unwelcome sexual conduct in the workplace that interferes with an employee's work performance or creates an intimidating, hostile, abusive or offensive work environment. Simple innuendo or sexual flirtation that may include vulgar language that is trivial or merely annoying would not create a hostile working environment. A company should, however, ban this type of activity from their workplace.

Sexual favoritism can play in the promotion of a female being granted such a promotion because she submits to unwelcome requests for sexual favors from a supervisor. If this occurs, both male and female co-workers can allege sexual harassment by showing that they were denied a chance at promotion, because of the sexual harassment directed toward the one female employee.

Employers can be held liable for harassing of non-employees, if the employer has some degree of control to stop this improper behavior and failed to do so.

Additionally, sexual harassment can violate the Civil Rights Act of 1964, if companies allow pinups, calendars, jokes, vulgar statements, innuendos, graffiti, and references to sexual activity.

After this review as to what constitutes sexual harassment in the workplace, we should turn our attention to preventing complaints.

It's important to recognize that the problem of sexual harassment can be "mitigated" rather than "litigated." Here are seven ways to avoid or limit liability of sexual harassment claims in your business:

• **Post the policy:** Establish a company policy prohibiting sexual harassment. Communicate it to all employees by posting it in common employee areas, such as the lunch room or vending machine area.

- Also, discuss the policy with managers, supervisors, and senior management
- Cover the policy during new employee orientation
- Discuss at time of transfers and promotions
- Discuss at employee meetings
- It should be discussed and become part of management committee meeting minutes
- Company newsletter
- Staff meetings

If your company has an employee handbook, a section of the book should be devoted to the company's sexual harassment policy. Discuss the consequences an offender will be subjected to, ranging from appropriate disciplinary action to discharge.

• **Procedures for filing a sexual harassment complaint:** Provide formal channels through which an employee can make a sexual harassment complaint. Be sure employees are familiar with the procedure, as well as who has been designated to address complaints. At least one of the designers should be a woman.

• **Treat every complaint seriously until proven otherwise:** Conduct a thorough investigation on every complaint. Document the response of the alleged harasser and warn the offender that harassment of any kind will not be tolerated. Take disciplinary action accordingly.

• **Training is a preventive measure:** Conduct regular employee meetings with managers to discuss measures to be taken when handling a complaint. Related company policies should be covered no less than semi-annually. Training should include distinguishing between friendly behavior and sexually harassing behavior. Stress to supervisors and managers that this is a serious matter, and the employee filing the complaint and those assisting with the investigation should not be retaliated against in any way.

- **Keep all investigation information confidential:** Information regarding a sexual harassment charge only needs to be discussed with those who are involved in responding to the complaint. During the investigation, ensure that names, quotes, dates, times and places are kept completely confidential.
- **Appoint a leader:** Establish guidelines for evaluating complaints. In organizations that do not have a human resource function, the line manager or president are usually the most appropriate people to act as coordinator of the process. The coordinator is responsible for providing a common thread of knowledge and participation throughout the entire process.
- **Treat employees equally:** Take prompt action to eliminate harassment upon determination that it occurred - no matter who the victim and no matter who the offender. Management must enforce its program evenhandedly, avoiding the tendency to be more lenient toward management than with workers.

The majority of companies prefer to resolve sexual harassment complaints without outside intervention. Following these suggestions will go a long way in managing this important issue.

Some reasons why Sexual harassment may not be reported are:

- Fear or losing one's job
- Anger
- Need for future references
- Depression
- Concern about being labeled a troublemaker
- Disgust
- Fear that they will be blamed for inviting the behavior
- Sadness
- Reluctance to invite public scrutiny of their private lives

Of those who have been victims of harassment, less than ten percent (10%) quit their jobs as a result of harassment. Another small group request a transfer in jobs to escape the situation.

Other issues regarding harassment can be costly to any organization when you include hiring costs and training associated with that new employee. Clearly then, the costs of sexual harassment in terms of lost productivity due to morale and turnover problems illustrates the necessity for organizations to prevent and control sexual harassment.

In conclusion, managers, supervisors and employees should be taught what to do to prevent harassment within their workplace to ensure that there is no chance of occurrence in your organization.

CHAPTER 9

EMPLOYER/EMPLOYEE RIGHTS

This Chapter prepared by

STEVEN B. WHEELER
Human Resource Consultant
Wheeler & Associates
Phoenix, MD 21131

Employers are required by various laws and regulations to maintain numerous records regarding you and every other worker that they employ. Some of these records include, but are not limited to:

- Health care plans
- Medical records
- ERISA/Pension
- Ethnic background
- Sex designation
- Payroll information
- Time cards/sheets
- Tax information
- OSHA records
- Immigration records
- Worker's compensation
- Safety records
- Injury and illness information

Generally, information collected by an employer should be of a business necessity, required by a specific regulation or job-related. In addition, some laws allow employers to collect certain information, but limit the manner in which they use it.

Many employers with Federal contracts are required to maintain an affirmative action plan and ask you to voluntarily identify yourself as a minority, veteran or your sex designation. This information should be done in a post-employment situation. Records requesting this information should be kept separate from other personnel records.

Different states have different laws concerning access to your personnel file. Also, these laws may limit your ability to review your file and under what circumstances, if any, you can request or make a copy of information contained in your file. Many states limit the frequency of your inspection of your own file and at what intervals and require that this review be done in the presence of a company representative.

Search and Seizure

Another issue is search and seizure and whether those areas, such as your locker or desk drawer as to whether you have a reasonable legitimate expectation of privacy in those areas. While the employer has interest in controlling losses in company property and inventory. There should be a policy posted and communicated to the employees regarding their exclusive province, but are the property of the company and, as such, are subject to search at their discretion. Your employer can't detain or confine you against your will while they call the police. However, they can discipline you appropriately if you leave work during working hours.

The Federal Employee Polygraph Protection Act of 1988 prohibits most private employers from requiring job applicants or employees to submit to a lie detector test, and even from requesting that they take one. Like most everything, there are exceptions to this law. Your employer may request a lie detector test if there is:

- Workplace theft for a specific incident
- You had access to the missing property

- There was reasonable suspicion that you were involved in the incident

Other exceptions are security companies who are engaged in handling, trading, transferring or storing currency and other forms of negotiable instruments. Lastly, drug and pharmaceutical companies whose applicants actually come into contact with controlled drugs.

A number of laws and government regulations require drug and alcohol testing for most federal contractors/employers who receive federal funding and both public and private transportation companies to have drug awareness programs.

Under the *Drug Free Workplace Act of 1988*, the federal government has most government contractors with greater than $25,000 in business to:

- Post a policy prohibiting drug use
- Establish drug awareness program
- Notify proper agency of employee drug conviction
- Require employees to notify them of a drug offense

Also, the *Department of Defense* (DOD) requires contractors to train and educate employees about drug abuse. There are certain positions that must be drug tested for security and health reasons.

Department of Transportation regulations require testing, including random, for virtually all safety-sensitive jobs in rail, sea, bus, air travel and maintenance to the actual operation. Issues that need to be addressed are:

- Employee consent
- Appropriate medical testing facility
- National Institute Drug Abuse (NIDA) certified
- Chain of Custody
- Medical Review Officer (MRO)
- Confirmatory tests
- Confidentiality of results

Two other Acts, *The Rehabilitation Act of 1973* and *Americans With Disabilities Act* (ADA) protect "qualified handicap". Current alcohol use or use of illegal drugs is not protected. So, if you are a current user of alcohol or drugs, an employer can refuse to hire you or can discipline or fire you, and you have no recourse to the protection of handicap laws.

The law recognizes the right of an employer to select and hire job applicants based on the usage of medical exams to include substance abuse testing procedures. An employer should protect your privacy rights by:

- Giving notice to all applicants prior to employment
- Make a job offer conditional on passing the drug test
- All applicants, regardless of sex, age, etc., are tested in the same job classification or job group

With regard to current employees, the employer should:

- Post their written drug policy
- Allow for appropriate grievance procedure for employees who refuse testing
- Does the company have reasonable suspicion for testing based on employee job performance
- Post accident testing that could present a danger to themselves or other employees

Under the Americans With Disabilities Act (ADA), job applicants can neither be asked if they have AIDS, nor be given an AIDS test, unless AIDS could be considered job related and of a business necessity. The jobs handling food like cook, waiter, waitress, meat packer are treated differently. An employer can refuse to hire someone with a communicable disease for a job handling food, if the disease can be transmitted by handling of such food. The Secretary of Health and Human Resources publishes a list annually to reflect current medical knowledge concerning what jobs are covered in the food industry. Your employer should offer an alternative position available that you are qualified to do, they should give you a chance to take that job.

Also, the results of any medical information or information concerning your medical condition or history must be kept on separate forms and in a file separate from your personnel records and must be kept confidential. There are specific limitations to who may be given access to your medical records. They are:

- Supervisor or manager with a need to know
- First aid or medical personnel
- Government officials investigating your employer's compliance

A number of state laws expressly allow you to request that your employer remove erroneous or dated information from your file and insist on an explanation of any document you disagree with and request that a change be made.

Surveillance and monitoring in the workplace is used to stimulate productivity, or to improve customer service and/or to decrease theft of company property, etc. Employers should determine if there are legitimate business reasons for obtaining this information, and they are legally entitled to have it.

The Federal Omnibus Crime Control and Safe Streets Act of 1968 prohibits intercepting wire, oral or electronic communications. The one exception is that employers can use extension phones to monitor employee "calls" in the course of ordinary business. They are required to hang up as soon as they determine that the call is personal.

The Privacy for Consumers and Workers Act of 1992 requires employers to tell workers when they are being monitored by computer, telephone, or any other method of surveillance, what kind of information is being gathered, and how it will be used. The information obtained must be directly relevant to an employee's job performance.

In addition, some laws allow employers to collect certain information, but restrict how they can use it. If a prospective employer seeks information about you from a credit bureau, the *Fair Credit Reporting Act* limits the employer's use of the information to be verified of previous employment. You must be told that the credit check will be made and that you have the right to find out the scope of the report and receive a copy. If you were denied a job or promotion, you must be told what part of the credit report played in that decision.

This is a general overview of some of the privacy issues for employers/employee and no intention was made to make this an all-inclusive review. You should get specific answers to other workplace privacy questions by reviewing the local or state statues where you operate your business or where you live.

CHAPTER 10

THE FOOD PLANT OFFICE AND THE OFFICE WORKER

There is a fine line between delegation and abdication of responsibility, you must follow up. You cannot just delegate authority and responsibility and then walk away from it.

The Office

The food plant office serves as the headquarters for the local food firm and is the center of all activities. It is the first place a new employee visits and its the first stop for all outsiders. The impression presented from this office is most important as it generally sets the tone for what follows. I have chosen this area of the food firm to describe in some detail the people that work in this office.

The Office Worker

The office worker that the new employee first meets or the public comes in contact with is the Head Secretary, Receptionist, Administrative Assistant, Manager, or Gal/Guy Friday. The impression they put forth whether it be by phone or by personal contact is most important.

The first thing they must remember is that they work for and represent someone else. If you truly believe any of the following statements you should never be working in an office:

1. It is degrading to work for someone else.

2. No one has the right to tell me what to do.

3. My boss is a more important/better person than I am.

4. My value comes only from pleasing and identifying with my boss.

5. If I were smarter/harder working, I would be a better person or I would be the boss instead of a secretary a receptionist, an Administrative Assistant, Manager, etc.

Your Job

The important thing about your job is that you have personal power:

You are an individual

You have confidence

You have courage

You have competence

You are the MANAGER of yourself.

Your job requires that you meet the needs of your employer and with a reasonable degree of loyalty, effort, and good will. You have a most unique position in the firm. You are in great demand. You earn reasonably good money. You are usually eligible for fringe benefits (medical, paid holidays and vacation, bonuses, retirement plans, etc.). Your hours and physical surroundings are safe and pleasant and your work is physically easy.

Your skills can be acquired at modest expense and they improve with time and practice. Your responsibility is limited, you do not have to take work home with you or give up your family and personal life in order to do your work.

You are a facilitator.

You get things done.

You cannot be dispensed with.

You must be a good communicator, that is, one that can effectively receive and transmit information. You should never look for trouble. You do not make assumptions, especially negative ones. You do not take anything for granted. You do not listen or participate in rumors. You do not start the 'grapevine'. You do not let anyone else speak for you.

You establish your own relationships. You use your strengths. You stay away from office diseases: Resentment, rigidity (its not my job), indifference, chronic boredom, and gossip.

You must have the following HARD SKILLS:

Type well (accurate, consistent, neat, and on time.)

Use office equipment proficiently.

Speak and listen well (good grammar, polite, and always a professional).

Write intelligently (clear, correct, concise, and organized.)

File accurately. The file system should follow the structure of the office and always be maintained in order, up-to-date. Further, you must know what to keep.

You, also, must have your own SOFT SKILLS:

Good judgment.

Flexible.

Discretion.

Sensitive to others.

Good sense of humor.

You must be a self motivator. You must be a leader. You must care about your work, your position, and your employer and his or her firm. You must always be alert to use your knowledge. You must make yourself indispensable. You must build your own self esteem.

You should always be a professional. Professionals never blame their mistakes on others. Professionals do not make excuses for poor work. Professionals do not take unnecessary shortcuts. Professionals do not get involved in personal vendettas or hold grudge or spread gossip. Finally, professionals do not put personal relationships before good performance.

Time and space permitting I would have liked to have taken each position in the food firm and write similar descriptions for each, however, one should be able to draw much from the above and apply it to most positions in a food firm.

CHAPTER 11

THE LEADER

The first responsibility of a leader is to define reality.
The last is to say 'thank you'.
In between, the leader is a servant. Max De Pree.

Why A Leader?

The first requirement in the success of any business is to have a CEO/COO (Chief Executive Officer/Chief Operation Officer) that is a leader. The Leader has 3 sources of power that goes with his position in the firm. The first source of power is the power of his position. The second source of power is his knowledge. And the third source of power is his personality. By developing knowledge and personality people will seek the leader out and seek his advice. Thus, the leader can use his formal power for fundamental change in leading the firm forward.

CEO was once defined as follows: The C stands for customer first, the E stands for employees second, and O stands for owners last. It really means if our products produced by our employees meet the customers expectations our owners will come out all right and they can expect a reasonable return on their investment due to the CEO's leadership.

Thus, the Chief Executive Officer or leader becomes a real coach/champion/cheer leader and the manager that has as his primary goal building people and products to make the business successful. People need a leader to keep everyone well informed at all times. Without clear and concise information, rumors start. Informed people do not rely on the grapevine for their information. They want a leader that is cooperative and not one that calls for compliance only. People look up to leadership, they need a mentor. They need a cheer leader to encourage them, that is, to tell them how they are doing. They need a coach to correct past errors and show them the right way. Further, they need this leader to be a manager of people and to communicate the firm's vision and values.

I recently read the following in a publication by Midwest Food Processors asking the question, "Are You Their Boss or Their Leader":

> A boss drives, a leader leads,
> A boss says "I", a leader says "We",
> A boss relies on authority, a leader relies on cooperation,
> A boss creates fear, a leader creates confidence,
> A boss knows how, a leader shows how,
> A boss creates resentment, a leader breathes enthusiasm,
> A boss fixes blame, a leader fixes mistakes,
> A boss makes work drudgery, a leader makes work interesting.

Functions Of A Leader Or The Manager

The three basic functions of a Leader are:

(1) to establish policy,
(2) to make decisions, and
(3) to exercise control over the operation.

Policy

Policy starts from the top down and its main purpose is to see that quality is built in from the bottom up. The first control over policies is to have them. Then it is a matter of seeing to it that they are expressed clearly; that those affected by them or responsible for their interpretation are supplied with copies of the policies; that they are kept appropriate by periodic review; that they are complied with; and finally, that either rules, regulations or procedures are developed for the execution of these policies.

Management

In making decisions management needs good intelligent data or information. Top management cannot personally observe the intimate details of the day to day operation and must base many of his decisions on reports from his subordinates. The more fully, systematically, and critically the information available to use in arriving at decisions, the better they will be made and the more confident you can be that they are the best decisions you can make toward achieving the objectives or goals. In some respects the problem of reporting is, in fact, the most difficult to resolve---what reports to require, how often the reports must be executed, and the methods that are taken to insure their accuracy.

One of the practical techniques in exercising control and reporting is based on PARETO'S CURVE. That is, in any series of elements to be controlled, a selected fraction (the vital few = 20%) always account for a large fraction in terms of effect(the trivial many = 80%). Examples of this concept are: Approximately 20% of your ingredients account for 80% of your costs, 20% of the quality characteristics account for 80% of the customers complaints, and 20% of the product defects account for 80% of the rejections, etc.

The Managers Job

The primary job of a manager is to give consistency of purpose and continuity to the organization. He is solely responsible to see that there is a future. Workers work in a system, but the manager works on the system. He sees to it that it produces the highest quality product at the lowest possible costs. No one else is responsible for the system as a whole and no one else is responsible for continuous improvement of the system. A successful manager relies on his staff to help make the many and necessary decisions as each staff member has specialized knowledge and interests and can focus in his area of expertise. All must be committed, visibly involved and project a leadership attitude. Below are some reasons why managers succeed:

1. They run results oriented rather than task oriented operations.

2. They concentrate on priorities and essentials.

3. They delegate.

4. They motivate their people to obtain desired results.

5. They work out realistic performance standards for all their people.

6. They structure their job first and then structure the entire organization to obtain the desired and expected results.

7. They maintain control.

8. They communicate.

9. They train their people to achieve results.

10. They translate all effective decisions into profitable actions.

This leader must have great stamina, be a role model for all to follow, provide motivational climate, give praise where it is deserved, and understand human behavior. He or she is a constant source of information and is always very secure.

Many of my cheer leaders, champions, coach, and leaders were my former professors or teachers or coaches. I have tried to emulate many of them over the years and the information I have imparted to my children, former students, and colleagues has been most sincere, directed, and always meant to provide the light that leads the way for them.

A personal note if you will. This year at Christmas I received a letter from a former student now heading up a major college food technology program in Turkey and he stated, "The news about your receiving the Appert Award made me very happy and, also, made me most proud of being one of your former students. Your picture hangs on my office wall and you have meant a great deal to me in my daily life in reaching the target effectively and safely...". Some people do not think of their teacher, or Professor as a Coach or Cheerleader, but if you would think back over some of the changes in your life you would have to agree that some of your teachers were just that.

Fundamentals Of Coaching/Teaching

As a former player and coach on a successful lacrosse and base ball team, I quickly learned there are certain fundamentals that one must understand:

Know what the tasks are that must be performed.

Know who is working on what tasks.

Know who can handle more tasks.

Know the skills of all of your people and how you can integrate them into a team to accomplish the firm's goal.

Players and coaches work hard at the above and when the talent, chemistry and physical ability is available, they can become winners.

Our whole goal as a teacher or coach should be to help people accept change, that is, to cope with the paradigm shifts that are taking place. We must lead the way. We must stick to the facts and show the advantages of any change. We must avoid downgrading past practices. We must follow up to prevent returning to old practices or work habits.

In handling any change we should remember what Kipling taught us:

"I had 6 honest men: they taught me all I knew. There names were *where,* and *what* and *when* and *why* and *how* and *who*" (Kipling).

I use these 5 W and 1 H for most problems and opportunities that I am confronted with and I find the answers to questions around the 5W1H usually gives me clues to the solutions and a future course to be taken.

As a teacher and coach I learned that there are certain steps that lead to success:

1. One must carefully explain the purpose and importance of what you are trying to teach.

2. One must carefully explain the process.

3. One must show how it is to be done.

4. One must observe while the person practices the process.

5. One must provide immediate and specific feedback (coach again or reinforce).

6. One must express confidence in the person's ability to be successful.

7. Lastly, one must agree on follow-up actions.

I have a little proverb that I like to use to illustrate the above principles:

"Tell me and I will forget,
Show me and I may remember,
but,
Involve me and I will understand"

In teaching, we use a lot of hands on or laboratory work as this laboratory work is the hands on approach. It is the same thing as the coach uses when working with the players during practice before the big game--take the time to show them how it should be done to make their job easier and better understood. Industry must apply the same principle if they want to see continuous improvement in their productivity, quality, and the bottom line.

Stating this another way, there are 5 steps of any coaching technique:

1. Get his or her agreement that a problem exists

2. Mutually discuss alternative solutions

3. Mutually agree on action to be taken to solve the problem(s)

4. Follow up to measure results, and

5. Recognize any achievement when it occurs

A good teacher or coach always works the following human relations commandments:

Call people by their name, preferably first name.

Smile (It takes 72 muscles to frown, but only 14 muscles to smile).

Be cordial and helpful.

Show them some interest (there is always some good in everybody).

Be generous with praise and cautious with criticisms.

Be considerate.

Be thoughtful.

Be alert to give of your service.

Difficult People

There are many people in today's World who appear to be difficult. Some of the reasons difficult people are the way they are as follows:

1. They are insecure

2. They lack experience

3. They are under tremendous pressure to satisfy

4. Past events frustrate them

5. Up to now, they may have been manipulated

6. They may have had some experiences that were most unsatisfactory

7. They really are the way they are because we let them be that way.

Everyone has something good to offer and as the leader, teacher or coach we must find that good and bring it out and help them to contribute.

Being Sensitive

As a teacher and a coach we need to be sensitive to our people. Being sensitive to people means the following to me:

We must have face to face communication.

We need to provide an ongoing training and development program for them.

We need to establish the right incentive program to bring them around.

We need to assure them of their future by developing job security programs.

Everyone has an invisible sign hanging from their necks: "make me feel important". Your face telegraphs how you feel. A smile costs nothing and it is contagious. We must learn to deal with what we were dealt. We must learn to get along with people (there is good in all of us). We must learn to enjoy other activities to lessen stress and relax.

We should all remember to be thankful for our problems, for if they were less difficult, someone with less ability would have our job. We should turn our disadvantages into advantages. We should always build for the tomorrow's.

Another proverb I like to quote:

"The man on top of the mountain didn't just fall there".

He got there because of hard work, responsive, hustle, and a lot of people along the way giving him help, encouragement, and support. We can all be winners and we can all reach the mountain top if we set our goals high and give it our best. In Figure 11.1 are my key attributes for the leader I want to work for and with.

FIGURE 11.1 - Gould's Key Attributes For My Leader

1. **Positive Attitude** - I want a leader who is positive about himself, about what he wants to be, about his point of view, and about his outlook on life, family, community, society, and the business world.

2. **Intelligent** - I want a leader who understands more than theory and facts. I want one who sees the practical side of the business and one who leads by being willing to change ahead of the times.

3. **Honesty** - I want my leader to be honest and above reproach. He must have great integrity and show it for all to see. He must have great tolerance for ambiguity, always objective, and most capable of making tough decisions. Further, he must have sound knowledge of and about the food business.

4. **Empathy** - I want my leader to have great feelings and ideas towards others. I want my leader to show this empathy through working with and through others.

5. **Decision Maker** - I want my leader to be a decision maker and willing to take risks to move the firm forward with vigor based on long range plans and goals using alternative routes at times. He must be an ambitious planner, aggressive and always oriented toward the future.

FIGURE 11.1 - Gould's Key Attributes For My Leader (Continued)

6. **Power** - I want my leader to have great starting power; but, more importantly, I want him to be self confident, show constant display of unwavering courage, yet be flexible enough to know when to change. I want him to be resilient, that is, have the power to bounce back. He must, also, have stress resistance, great energy, always enthusiastic, and display the willingness to always cooperate. He must be self aware and be a great self-disciplinarian.

7. **Responsible** - I want my leader to be responsible for himself, his firm, his people, his community, and his industry. He must have great recall ability and have the intuition to look to the future to solve problems. He must have ability to set priorities on himself, his work, and his firm.

8. **Love** - I want a leader that has great love for his job, his people and his industry that extends beyond his family and community convictions. I want my leader to enjoy his work and display that enjoyment, enthusiasm, and inherent energy for all to see and hear.

9. **Visibility** - I want my leader to always be visible. I want him to manage by walking around (MBWA). I want my leader to have great vision for the firm and the future of it, be self confident and have the ability to work through and with all of his people. I want him to give his people goals and a strong sense of direction. He must set the example for all others to emulate. He must practice the rule of praise in public, but only criticize in private. Further, should always give credit when credit is due.

10. **Communicator** - I want my leader to be a great communicator. Communication is much more than speaking or talking or writing or pictures or charts, or other visual aides. It is listening, it is eye contact, and it is body language. Communicating is a great art and sincerity is most vital to the person(s) you are communicating with.

CHAPTER 12

TEAMS

"No one of us is as smart as all of us"
and
"Two heads are always better than one"

Today, there is a new approach in the modern food firm, that is, the development and deployment of teams. Developed teams have goals not for the individual as such, but for the team and the firm.

Types Of Groups Working For The Good Of The Whole

There are many descriptions of groups of people working together. One of the first and still effective in some areas the so called committee system. Committees generally serve as an investigative body or group of people to report after completing their investigation to a higher body or the group that appointed them for further action. Committees are seldom empowered to follow through, however they are valuable to their superiors if operated properly. If not operated properly, I have to agree with Will Rogers when he stated, "Outside of traffic there is nothing that has held this country back as much as committees".

Some firms use "Task Force" with people assigned to a group to solve departmental or process lines. Many task forces may last too long and become quite ineffective in the long run because they have no real goal. The food industry may use task forces, but they are nearly always management driven and the worker as a member of the task force is only a follower. I believe task forces are quite acceptable, but they must be properly structured and operated correctly to be effective and helpful.

Some 15 years ago Quality Circles were the rage. A quality circle is a small group of volunteer people and a supervisor working together to solve carefully selected problems. They are most effective for their intended use and they set the stage for employees to work with management in solving plaguing problems. They devote most of their time to productivity and quality problems and generally make outstanding contributions. Some firms still use quality circles and report excellent results in bringing the worker together with management.

Another effective group is the Project Group. These people are put together because of the need to develop a new process, a new product, a new package, a new facility, etc. This group again is temporary, but very effective because it cuts across departmental lines and it represents several facets of the firm. The project group has a very specific mission and when this is accomplished they are usually dissolved.

Teams are a group of people working together to reach an established goal, usually established by the team. The team members quickly learn to collaborate with each other because they identify with the team goal. They learn to cooperate and eliminate personal competitiveness for the good of the team and its goal. They learn to communicate and share their talents, their strengths, and their resources. Further, they make decisions by consensus and, thus, they all become very committed. Most importantly, they learn to keep score and always know where the goal is whether it be improved quality, line efficiency, improved productivity, or just plain winning.

Types Of Team Players

There are four types of team players: Contributors, Collaborators, Communicators, and Challengers according to "Team Players and Teamwork".

The Contributors are task-oriented. They do their homework, providing the team with technical information and push for higher standards. They are most dependable.

The Collaborators are goal-directed. Give them a mission and they're flexible and open to new ideas even if it means working in an area outside their defined role. They are the big-picture people.

The Communicators are process-oriented. The are good listeners and can resolve conflicts and facilitate action by building consensus.

The Challengers question the goals and the method, and even the ethics of the team. They are willing to disagree with higher authority and encourage the team to take risks. They are valued for their candor and openness.

The individual team member must be capable of being a good listener. Each team member must have great trust, respect and learn to cooperate with each other.

Team Objectives

The teams primary objective is to solve problems and to do this the team must have an action plan--the goal--and they must have a planned time to meet. To be effective, the team must have a leader to conduct the meeting. The team must have a facilitator, that is, a person that makes it easy for them to keep moving forward. The team must have a recorder, that is, a person to keep score. Finally, the team must have a resource person--someone to provide facts and information relevant to its needs as it moves toward the goal.

Team Building

Team building is simply a process in which several diverse individuals are bonded together as a team. This autonomous work group has a great attitude, they are enthusiastic, and they are productive.

Teams prevent isolation.

Teams build moral.

Teams achieve success.

Teams become loyal to the firm and all that it stands for.

Teams develop esprit de corps.

In addition, teams do the following for their firm:

1. They reduce absenteeism
2. They improve communication
3. They build self esteem
4. They commit to quality and the customer
5. They improve productivity
6. They increase morale
7. They develop family feeling, that is, we can attitude.

All teams need the following:

A. A mission statement--"why are we meeting together or what is the goal of this team".

B. Operating principle, that is, the culture of the team, the things they will do, and how they will proceed. One must clearly understand that teams have to be empowered to be effective. Empowerment is all about letting go by management so the team can get going towards their objective, the goal.

C. An action plan, that is, agreement on the approach they use to accomplish their objective(s), in other words, a detailed listing of the steps to achieve their goal.

For a team to become effective, the following must be clearly spelled out -

Team Membership

Who is going to be a member of the team? Who is interested in the work of the team? Membership on a team is a responsibility.

It is based on ones interest, area of expertise, and willingness to work as a team member toward reaching the goal. Proper skills are needed to solve problems, to make decisions, and to take action and every team member must want to participate and make a contribution.

Team Meetings

Team meetings are always on company time and generally the team members are given, at least, one hour per week to work on the objectives of the team to reach their goal. Obviously, the time and place of any meeting has to be flexible and suitable for the membership of the team.

Training

Training, whether it be people skills, technical skills, or administrative skills must be made available at the right teachable moment. It must be relative to the needs. It must be appropriate for the people. And it must be adequate to fulfill their needs.

Kinds Of Teams

There are many kinds of teams in use today depending on the kind and size of the firm. Examples of some of my favorite teams are:

EITS, that is, Employee Involvement Teams

QITS, that is, Quality Improvement Teams

OFIT, that is, Opportunities for Improvement Teams

CATS, that is, Corrective Action Teams

PATS, that is, Process Analysis Teams

PITS, that is, Process Improvement Teams

A description of the work of these teams should not be necessary as the title is quite self expressive. However, looking at the PITS team, the whole idea is to obtain better process control and improvement. Process improvement is based on the teams thinking as follows:

We accept our responsibilities.
We share information with each other.
We know the requirements of our operation.
We prevent problems from happening.
We are responsible for our operation.
We can be held accountable.
We perform at optimum efficiency 100% of the time.
We have vision for the future for our firm.
We will continue to make measurable improvements for the good of our firm.
We care.

In summary, it must be emphasized that when we empower an individual or a team, they automatically accept the responsibility and they should be trusted and held accountable. These are trusts that go with the territory and they are very basic to understanding what empowerment really means.

FIGURE 12.1 - What Is A Team?

WHEN you find yourself part of a group of people who are equally committed to the same mission,

WHEN you see that you are appreciated for your special qualities,

WHEN you know that fellow team members care about you and your performance as much as they care about their own,

WELL that's better than any machine.

ITS A TEAM!

T. L. Brown, IW March 2. 1992

FIGURE 12.2 - Characteristics of Effective and Ineffective Teams*

ATTRIBUTE	EFFECTIVE TEAMS	INEFFECTIVE TEAMS
Information	Flows freely, down, & sideways Full Sharing Open and Honest	Flows mainly down, weak horizontally Hoarded, withheld Used to build power, Incomplete, mixed messages
People relationships	Trusting Respectful Collaborative Supportive	Suspicious & Partisan Pragmatic, based on need, liking Competitive Withholding
Conflict	Regarded as natural, even helpful On issues, not persons	Frowned on and avoided Destructive Involves personal traits & motives
Atmosphere	Open Nonthreatening Noncompetitive Participative	Compartmentalized Intimidating Guarded Fragmented, closed groups
Decisions	By consensus Efficient use of resources Full commitment	By majority vote or forcing Emphasis on power Confusion and dissonance
Creativity	More options Solution oriented	Controlled by power subgroups Emphasis on activity & inputs
Power base	Shared by all On competence Contribution to team	Hoarded On politicking, alliances Pragmatic sharing Contribution to power source

FIGURE 12.2 - Characteristics of Effective and Ineffective Teams* - Continued

ATTRIBUTE	EFFECTIVE TEAMS	INEFFECTIVE TEAMS
Motivation	Commitment to goals set by team Belong, i.e., needs satisfied More chance for advancement through group	Going along with imposed goals Coercion and pressure Personal goals ignored Individual achievement valued without concern for the group
Rewards	Based on contribution to group Peer recognition	Based on unclear system Based on subjective, often arbitrary appraisals

* Taken from T.L. Quick. 1992 Successful Team Building. American Management Association

CHAPTER 13

MEETINGS

This is a story about four people named Everybody, Somebody, Anybody, and Nobody. There was an important job to be done, and Everybody was sure Somebody would do it. Anybody could have done it. Nobody did it. Somebody got angry, because it was Everybody's job. Everybody thought Anybody could do it, but Nobody realized Everybody wouldn't do it. So Everybody blamed Somebody when Nobody did what Anybody could have done! (taken from Forbes magazine).

Some people refer to meetings as a place where you take minutes and waste hours. No meeting should ever be a waste of time if it is planned well in advance and the right people are in attendance. However, poor meetings do occur because we do not know the objective of the meeting, that is, there is no single focus. Or the meeting is delayed because someone did not arrive on time and all the others were punished who did arrive on time and thus, the mood of all was strained.

Meetings are intended to psyche-up the attendees for whatever the task that lies as the focus of the meeting. Meetings are intended as a place to convey important information, to collect information, to study problems, or to implement a solution to a given problem. All meeting should involve each attendee in one way or another.

The following are my suggestions for better meetings:

Before The Meeting

1. Schedule the place for the meeting

2. Establish the time for the meeting

3. Determine how the room should be set-up, that is, classroom, Block "O", "U", "Y", theater, etc.

4. Determine what visual aides will be needed, that is, chalk board, flip chart, screen and projector (35 mm, Overhead, Video, Movie, etc.), podium, microphone including number and type, head table, platform (height and location)

5. Inform all attendees with appropriate announcement along with prepared agenda.

6. Place note pads with pencil or pen at each station

7. Request ice water and glasses or soft drinks at each station along with napkin.

At The Start Of The Meeting

1. If not previously appointed or selected, appoint a chair to conduct the meeting

2. If not previously appointed or selected, appoint recorders:

   A. Handle chalk board, flip chart, audio visuals

   B. Record the minutes of the meeting and publish them immediately following the meeting and distribute to all attendees and others needing the record

3. Select a facilitator to assist is the progress of the meeting.

4. Select a Resource person to provide the needed facts or other information

5. Obtain agreement on Proposed Agenda and make necessary corrections at outset of meeting

6. Obtain agreement on the "ground rules" at the start of the meeting, that is, Robert's Rules of Order, etc.

7. Clarify the purpose of the meeting, that is what problem(s) and/or opportunities are on the agenda

8. Establish a time limit for the meeting, and if necessary, the time limit for anyone to speak at any given time

9. Agree on how the meeting will be conducted, that is,

   A. Brainstorm session--Out pouring of ideas

   B. Cause and Effect diagram with Cards

   C. Pareto Analysis--determination of 'vital few' and 'trivial many'

   D. Project planning process including flow chart to identify critical control points and allowable deviations with descriptions and possible causes versus true causes

   E. Show and Tell session with flip charts, visuals and/or outside speaker, video, movie, or demonstration of specific equipment.

During The Meeting

1. Is the agenda kept visible and followed at all times

2. Is the leader chairing the meeting or participating and/or monopolizing the meeting

3. Is everyone involved in the discussion

4. Are agreements established before on different parts of the agenda

5. Are the following issues covered, that is, 5W1H

   a. What must be done and will resources be required?
   b. Why must it be done?
   c. When must it be done?
   d. Where will the various steps be performed?
   e. How will the changes be monitored?
   f. Who will do each task?

6. At the end of the meeting, did the Leader summarize the action plan?

7. Are plans clear as to any follow up meetings, including time, place, agenda, needed information to be gathered, etc.

Meetings are an important part of any team or group activity. The above is a good starting place, but must be refined and adapted to fit the needs of the group or team holding the meeting.

My rules for a team to win are:

1. Know the game plan, that is, what is the objective

2. Always play by the rules

3. Learn to keep score using the "Q" tools

4. Have fun while you meet and, always

5. Play to win.

Teams should always be action oriented. They must want to meet to improve their work. Their reward comes from seeing the results, that is, the winning score.

CHAPTER 14

TEAMS AND THEIR "Q" TOOLS

"The will to win is not nearly as important as the will to prepare to win". - Bobby Knight

Winning

The will to win is through people. As previously stated, people make a company. All decisions and plans are made by people. Work is done by people. People who feel good about themselves, do good work and produce the intended results. The following are some characteristics of winning teams:

1. They learn to solve problems
2. They have great leadership
3. Every team member is a participant
4. They make decisions
5. Each member knows what role they are playing and thus, they have no internal conflicts because they set their own agenda and climate as a team.
6. They know what their goal is and by keeping score they make sure they reach it.

7. They are very communicative, that is, they constantly ask questions, they listen for answers and ideas, and they all focus on what is being said.

8. They look for positive opportunities for continuous improvement and performance for the good of the firm.

9. They are highly motivated and they feel good about themselves.

10. Each member of the team feels that he is an important part of the whole, i.e., he connects to their team. He has high self esteem, great energy output, and performs at top level for the good of the whole team.

11. Most importantly, the team produces results that lead to continuous improvement as continuous improvement is only achieved through people.

Team Tools

A team needs tools to accomplish the work of the team to reach the goal. These tools are what every firm must recognize and use for continuous improvement. We must measure and we must keep score or we will never know if we have reached the goal or won.

In my book on Total Quality Management, I have given a complete discussion of the 7 "Q" Problem Solving Tools and how to Design Experiments to evaluate new machines, new ingredients, new methods, etc. I will not repeat the above details here except to summarize some of the information as the team must have knowledge of these tools for success.

In Figure 14.1, I have shown how these tools can be used to solve problems and help a team do its work.

A team is generally formed because a problem exists or an opportunity for improvement has been suggested. The first requirement of any team is to establish a goal, what is the problem, where should the control be, what caused the inferior product, when did it occur, how can it be corrected, who is responsible, and where are the numbers to know the depth of the problem? Answers to these questions may take much time and the answers must be supported by actual data.

FIGURE 14.1 - Team Problem Solving Model

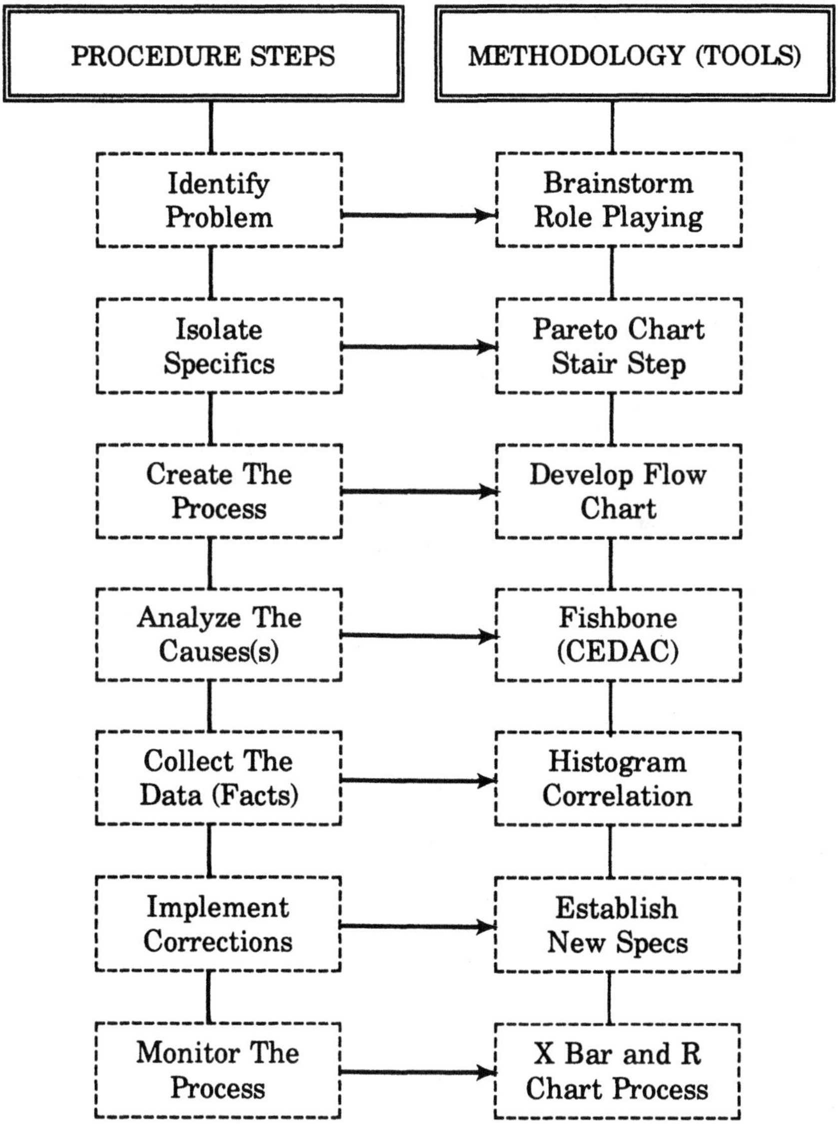

The second requirement for problem solving by teams is that each team member must have their own "Q" tool box to keep score and interpret the data or the numbers. Data interpretation tell us if we are winning. In my opinion, eye balling of a production line is really useless if we wish to know if we are keeping up with the competition and if we are really showing any improvement. Industry needs to understand data interpretation.

In the real world today instruments with automatic charting of the data are readily available; however, before anyone can understand the use of and interpretation of automated data they should have a 'feel' for the data by working the numbers through the "Q" tools in their personal tool box. If they do not know how to use their own "Q" tools, they may be interpreting something that is not relevant or useful to them through some of the automated instrumentation.

The following are brief outlines of how each tool could be used.

A. Brainstorming - Problem Solving "Q" Tool No. 1

There are four basic rules for success with brainstorming:

(1) New ideas are created without judging the merits of any idea,

(2) Freewheeling is emphasized, that is, anything goes, the wilder the idea, the better it may be,

(3) Ideas may be hitch hiked off some one else's idea, and

(4) The goal is to try for quantity, in other words create as many ideas as possible.

<u>Procedure to follow with brainstorming problem solving:</u>

1. Identify the problem by writing a clear description of the problem on a flip chart or chalk board for everyone to clearly see at all times,

2. Select a Leader to keep the session moving,

3. Select a Recorder to record all suggestions on the flip chart or the chalk board,

4. The Leader asks each person, one at a time, to offer an idea or cause of the problem. Everyone should be given a chance by going around the table or room, one person at a time. Each person should only give one idea at a time. The idea is to get everyone involved, thus, using the team approach,

5. No idea should be evaluated or thrown out. Free wheeling is the name of the problem solving tool. Most importantly, any unrelated idea should be encouraged. Ideas may come from hitch hiking off someone elses idea.

6. Questions are allowed, but only for clarification purposes. No one should be permitted to interrupt, or censor, or criticize,

7. Members of the team can pass on their turn, but can always add ideas on later turns.

8. When everyone passes on a complete turn, the brainstorm session is over.

9. The idea list is turned over to a problem solving team, such as Pareto, and they follow up by generating data to interpret the cause of the problem.

An example of a brainstorming problem is shown in Figure 14.2 with the causes of the problem coming forth from the panel members.

FIGURE 14.2 - Why Do We Always Have Problems With Quality?

Poor raw materials

Equipment worn out and/or not controllable

No process control limits established

No in-line or on-line controls

No cooperation from Quality Assurance

Methods of process are not clearly established

Insufficient manpower

Management says "run it"

No actual data taken to know if good or bad

Employees take no interest--no team effort

B. Pareto - Problem Solving "Q" Tool No. 2

The Pareto principle describes the way causes occur in nature and/or human behavior. The Pareto principle tells us that 80% of the problems come from 20% of the causes. The Pareto principle helps to separate the 'vital few' from the 'trivial many' (Figure 14.3). The data for a Pareto analysis may come from a Brainstorming session or from actual reports or data generated by the Pareto team.

A typical problem might be, WHERE DO COMPLAINTS COME FROM FOR OUR POTATO CHIPS?

The following are the steps to be followed to solve this problem using the Pareto technique.

1. Identify the type of complaints by the frequency in which they are reported from actual records or from a brainstorming session, that is,

Type of Complaint	Frequency/Complaints
Off-flavor	30
Rancid	20
Off Color	10
Poor Texture	8
Too Oily	7
Too Salty	4
Not Enough Salt	3
Too Many Broken-Hash	2
Opening of Bag	1
TOTAL COMPLAINTS	85

2. Calculate the frequency of each complaint as a percent of the total number of complaints as follows:

Complaint	Frequency	Percent Frequency
Off Flavor	30	35.3
Rancid	20	23.5
Off Color	10	11.8
Poor Texture	8	9.4
Too Oily	7	8.2
Too Salty	4	4.7
Not Enough Salt	3	3.5
Too Many Broken	2	2.4
Opening of Bag	1	1.2
TOTAL	85	100

3. Calculate the percent cumulative frequency in descending order as shown below:

Complaint	Frequency	% Frequency	Cumulative Frequency In %
Off Flavor	30	35.3	35.3
Rancid	20	23.5	58.8
Off Color	10	11.8	70.6
Poor Texture	8	9.4	80.0
Too Oily	7	8.2	88.2
Too Salty	4	4.7	92.9
Not Enough Salt	3	3.5	96.4
Too Many Broken	2	2.4	98.8
Opening of Bag	1	1.2	100.0

4. These data can be plotted on a Pareto Diagram Chart as shown in Figure 14.3. The first three complaints are considered the "Vital Few" and all the others are the "Trivial Many" simply because some 70% of the complaints are related to these three causes. Thus, these are the complaints to work on first to solve the complaint problem. This does not mean the others are not of some importance, but it would be a waste of money to work on the bag or hash problem when the major complaints are flavor, rancidity and off color.

Some people in working with Pareto charts add the dollar value of the product to the vertical axis to bring the data into clear focus for management and their better understanding of the problem. Pareto is an excellent "Q" tool to assist management in making decisions. In the example cited, management should do, at least, three things immediately if they wish to lower consumer complaints:

Flavor is without a doubt directly related to rancidity, therefore, reduce the shelf life of the package by using "use before date" on the bag, use nitrogen as a gas flush instead of air, and/or develop better control procedures on the breakdown of the oil in the fryer.

The color problem is directly related to the quality of potatoes used to manufacture the chips or the frying procedures in use.

Not all problems are this simple, but you must know where to start before assigning causes and Pareto gives us this opportunity in a process control procedure.

FIGURE 14.3 - Pareto Diagram - Consumer Complaints

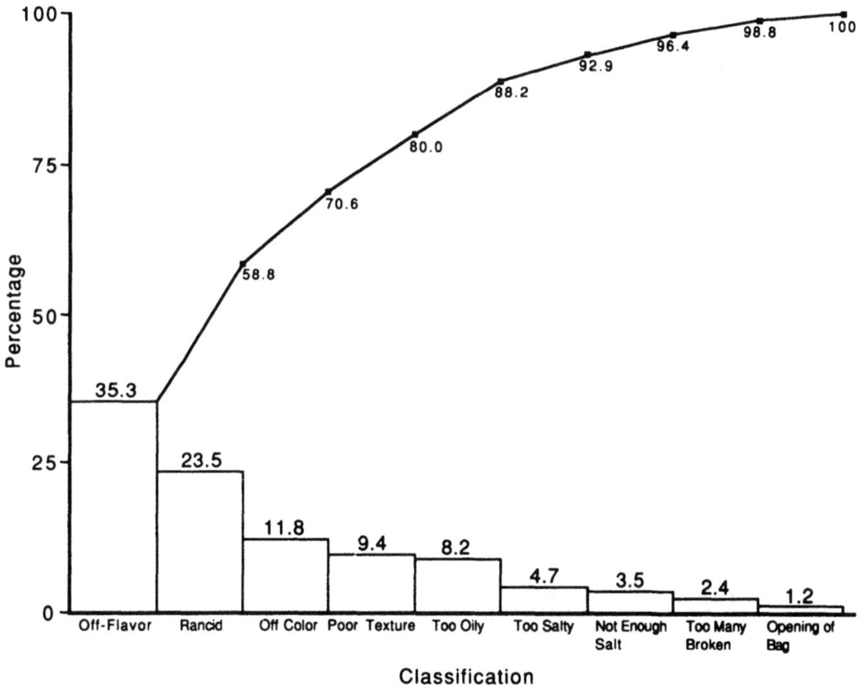

Note: Off-flavor, rancid and off-color are the "vital few" and all the other causes are the "trivial many".

C. Frequency Distributions, Histograms, Probability Plots, Specifications, And Capability Index Problem Solving Using "Q" Tool No. 3

Variations exist and all variations exist according to a definite pattern. These patterns are sometimes called frequency distributions. If they are normal variations, the data when plotted will resemble a bell or be bell shaped and, thus if we continue to take data from the same lot or population, the curve will repeat itself. Generally the measurements will cluster around the middle or center of the curve and we call this type of curve a normal distribution or curve. Other shapes of data when plotted tell us a lot about the actual data.

Another way to treat data is to make a histogram. This is a bar chart showing the variations or distribution of the observations. It is a powerful tool for elementary analysis. To describe the distribution of data, we need two measurements. One for the central tendency or the mean or average and the other for its dispersion, that is, the range or standard deviation (the largest value minus the smallest value). The mean identifies the location of the center of the distribution and the standard deviation describes the variations from the mean. Also, the standard deviation describes the shape of the curve and it is used to interpret the data, that is plus or minus 1 standard deviation = 68% of the total data, 2 standard deviations = 96% of the data, and 3 standard deviations = 99.7% of the data or total area under the curve. (Figures 14.4, 14.5 and 14.6).

A process capability plot shows us the full range of the data or the spread of the process and is targeted at 6 standard deviations (plus or minus 3 standard deviations). This number tells us what the process is capable of doing.

The specification width or limit may be added and should be somewhat larger than the normal spread or process variation. The specification width or limit is set by the customer as the functional requirements. It tells us what characteristics our product must have to meet the customers expectations.

The process limits are due to the inherent variation of the process due only to common causes. The process is said to be in control when only the source of variation is from common causes. The capability of the process is determined by the total variation that comes from common causes.

FIGURE 14.4 - A Normal Bell Curve

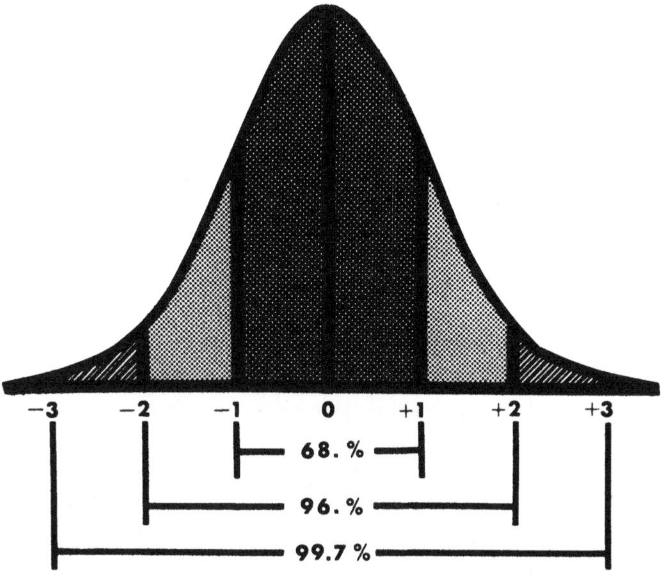

FIGURE 14.5 - Expected Weight Distribution Of Product In Control And Underweight

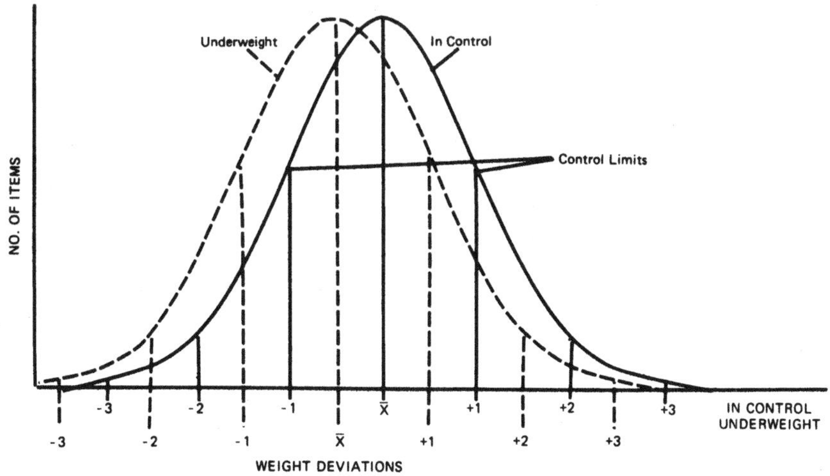

Note: $\overline{X}$ is the target weight

FIGURE 14.6 - Frequency Distribution For Measured Variable

Class Interval (Value) (c)	Frequency	f	d	fd	fd^2	%	Cumulative Frequency in % Ascending	Descending
18	1	1	-4	-4	16	0.5	0.5	100.0
19	~~1111~~ ~~1111~~	10	-3	-30	90	5.0	5.5	99.5
20	~~1111~~ ~~1111~~ ~~1111~~ ~~1111~~ ~~1111~~ ~~1111~~ 111	33	-2	-66	132	16.5	22.0	94.5
21	~~1111~~ ~~1111~~ ~~1111~~ ~~1111~~ ~~1111~~ ~~1111~~ ~~1111~~ ~~1111~~ ~~1111~~ ~~1111~~ ~~1111~~	55	-1	-55	55	27.5	49.5	78.0
22	~~1111~~ ~~1111~~ ~~1111~~ ~~1111~~ ~~1111~~ ~~1111~~ 1	31	0	0	0	15.5	65.0	50.5
23	~~1111~~ ~~1111~~ ~~1111~~ ~~1111~~ 11	22	1	22	22	11.0	76.0	35.0
24	~~1111~~ ~~1111~~ ~~1111~~ 11	17	2	34	68	8.5	84.5	24.0
25	~~1111~~ ~~1111~~ 1	11	3	33	99	5.5	90.0	15.5
26	~~1111~~ 111	8	4	32	128	4.0	94.0	10.0
27	~~1111~~ 1	6	5	30	150	3.0	97.0	6.0
28	111	3	6	18	108	1.5	98.5	3.0
29	11	2	7	14	98	1.0	99.5	1.5
30	1	1	8	8	64	0.5	100.0	0.5
Z=22	S (Total)	200		36	1030	100.0		

1. *Standard Deviation* (68%) $s = c\sqrt{\frac{Sfd^2}{f} - \left(\frac{Sfd}{f}\right)^2} = 1\sqrt{\frac{1030}{200} - \left(\frac{36}{200}\right)^2} = \sqrt{5.15 - .0324} = \sqrt{5.1176} = 2.26$

2. *Standard Deviation* (95%) $2s = 4.52$

3. *Standard Deviation* (99%) $3s = 6.78$

X (Average) $= Z + \frac{c \times Sfd}{Sf} = 22 + \frac{1 \times 36}{200} = 22 + .18 = 22.18$

CV (Coefficient of Variability) $= \frac{s}{x} \times 100 = \frac{2.26}{22.18} \times 100 = .102 \times 100 = 10.2\%$

It may represent as much as 6 standard deviations. The customer may expect much less variation in the products that they buy. Thus, one would conclude that a process that has up to 6 standard deviations is not capable of complying with most customer expectations. Therefore, one must know the capability of a process. This is called the "capability index" and is determined by dividing the specification width by the process width. The higher the number, the more capable the process. The capability index is a good measure of the "health" of the process.

A probability plot is often used to test the capability of the process. It is a measure of estimating how well the measurements used to make the average and range chart fit the normal curve. It, also, estimates the shape of the distribution. It is a graph of the cumulative percentages from a frequency table.

Frequency Distributions, Histograms, Probability Plots, Specifications, and Capability Index are used to summarize data and to tell a factual story regarding a process or measurements of a process.

D. Flow Charting - Problem Solving "Q" Tool No. 4

The process flow chart or diagram visually shows how an item or product moves through the system and WHO and WHAT acts upon or interacts with it, that is, the events that occur. It is literally a picture of the process in diagram form. A process flow diagram should show the various critical control points in the process that may have an impact on the final quality of the product.

A process flow diagram is almost mandatory under the proposed Hazard Analysis and Critical Control Point(HACCP) Regulation from USDA and FDA. The flow chart in Figure 14.7 for potato chips is an example of how Critical Control Points can be identified. The use of this chart is the first thing a process team must learn to use. It should be part of the 'handbook' of each line employee so that they can see the forest from the trees. They should see how their unit operation ties into the line and what lack of control could do to the entire line. A team starts with this information and develops data (assuming that the firm does not have any) and learns to interpret whether or not the process is in control, that is, is the unit operation within

FIGURE 14.7 - Potato Chip Manufacture With Quality Assurance And Control Areas Enumerated For Each Unit Operation

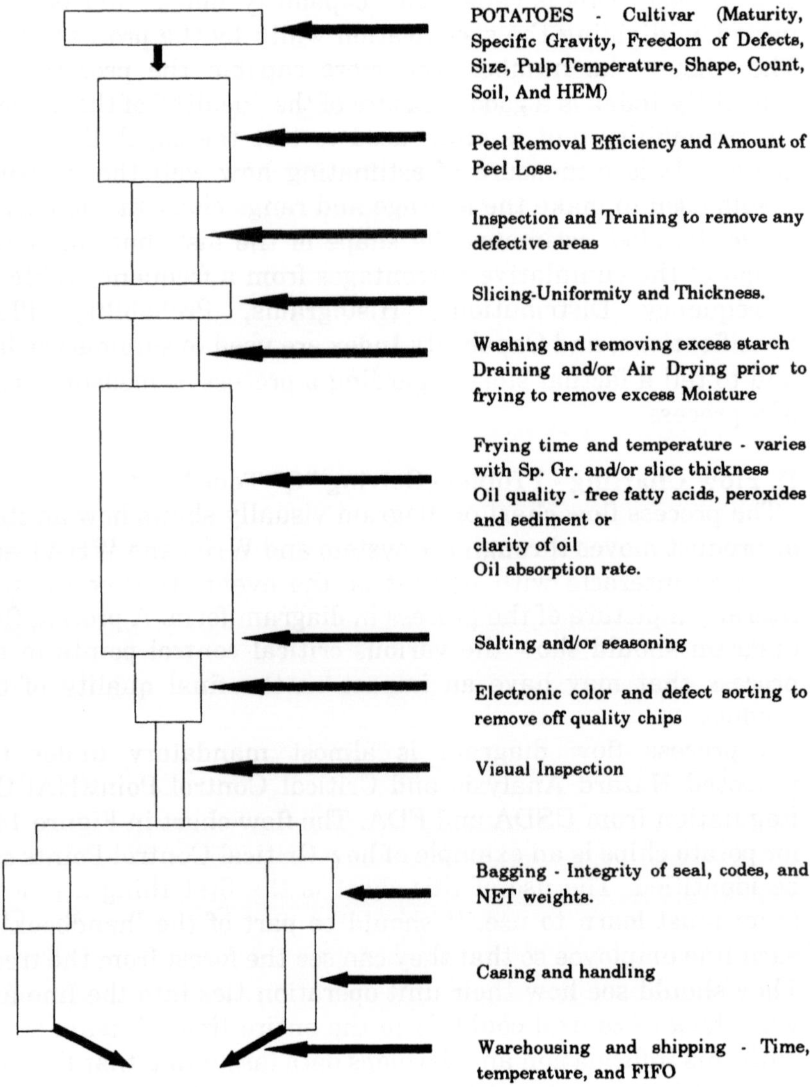
POTATOES - Cultivar (Maturity, Specific Gravity, Freedom of Defects, Size, Pulp Temperature, Shape, Count, Soil, And HEM)
Peel Removal Efficiency and Amount of Peel Loss.
Inspection and Training to remove any defective areas
Slicing-Uniformity and Thickness.
Washing and removing excess starch Draining and/or Air Drying prior to frying to remove excess Moisture
Frying time and temperature - varies with Sp. Gr. and/or slice thickness
Oil quality - free fatty acids, peroxides and sediment or
clarity of oil
Oil absorption rate.
Salting and/or seasoning
Electronic color and defect sorting to remove off quality chips
Visual Inspection
Bagging - Integrity of seal, codes, and NET weights.
Casing and handling
Warehousing and shipping - Time, temperature, and FIFO

tolerances or specifications that have been previously developed or established. If not, why not. Keeping the flow chart up to date with all the CCP's enumerated is most critical and, of course, having numbers to establish that the line is in control is most relevant.

The benefits of flow charting can be summarized as follows:

1. The worker becomes more familiar with the entire process,

2. Management can make the necessary changes or improvements as dictated by the capability index for any given unit operation,

3. There is greater communication among the team members when each can see the whole process,

4. The employees become more enthusiastic supporters of quality efforts when they know the capability of each unit operation, and
5. Productivity can be greatly enhanced and much waste can be reduced by taking advantage of the flow chart and what is actually happening at each unit operation.

E. Cause And Effect Diagram with Cards - Problem Solving "Q" Tool No. 6.

Cause and Effect Charting (CEDAC) is a simple technique for dissecting a problem or process. CEDAC identifies all possible relationships among INPUT and OUTPUT variables, that is, the five causes of variations in an operation (Materials, Machinery, Manpower, Methods, and Environment). CEDAC organizes the thinking and provides a plan of attack all at the same time.

Many times it is essential for the team to use a Cause and Effect Diagram with Cards (CEDAC) to pin point problem areas (see Figure 14.8). This is often called the "Fishbone Chart" simply because any identified bone may be the cause of a given effect one is attempting to isolate. Some firms use large wall mounted "fishbone diagrams" as illustrated in Figure 14.8 and locate this in the area where the workers can fill out a card indicating where they think the problem is. These cards are then pinned to the specific point on the chart and after a given time, the team removes the chart and the cards and brainstorms all the major and minor causes to the problem. The data are then ranked using Pareto to arrive at the "Vital Few" and the "Trivial Many". The committee next votes on which particular contributor or attribute to start generating data to establish their theorized solution to the problem. Once they have pin pointed the problem area with their data, they then establish new controls and move on to other problem areas, should they exist.

FIGURE 14.8 - Example Of CEDAC For Potato Chip Manufacture

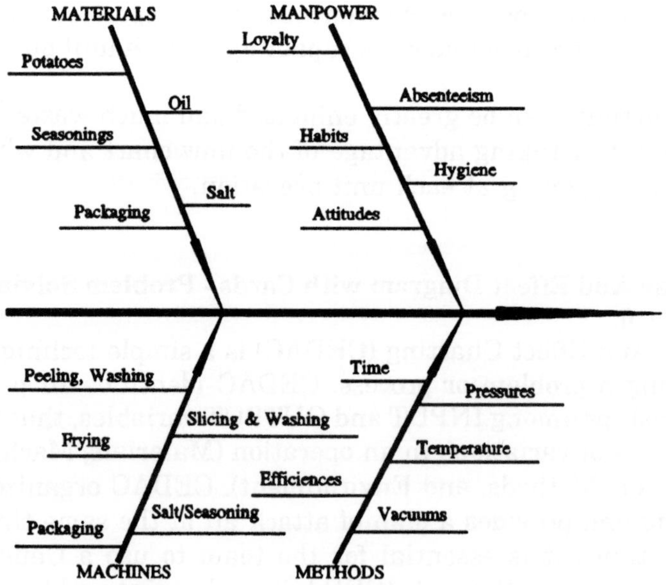

F. Run Chart (Variable Or Attribute Charting Or X Bar And R Chart Development - Problem Solving "Q" Tool No. 7.

The run chart is often called the control chart or the X Bar and R chart. (See Figure 14.9 for example X Bar and R Chart). It is a tool used to study the variation in a repetitive process. It is literally a stretched out histogram. The run chart provides an effective means of continuously monitoring a repetitive process. The data once plotted on the chart tells the operator what the process is doing, it is actually a talking picture of the process. The run chart gives the operator an in-line control tool of the on-going process. It tells the operator if the process is within or outside of the specification limits. The run chart tells management how to distinguish between special causes and common causes. (Common causes are the faults of the system, representing some 80 to 85% of the problems and they are the responsibility of management to improve. The special causes are assignable to chance, that is, materials, machines, methods, man, or the environment that may cause the problem. The special causes can be traced down and eliminated. They represent some 15 to 20% of the problems and generally are the responsibilities of the operator to correct).

Run charts are only as good as the interpretation of the data. The operator must understand the calculation and use of the average, the range, upper control limit for the average and range, and lower control limit for the average. The operator should understand the Zone System, that is, dividing the control limits into 6 standard deviations about the mean or average. One plus or minus standard deviation should be the red area, meaning the process should be stopped if two out of three successive points are outside the control limits as the process is out of control. The next zone should be marked the yellow area or caution zone. This area is plus or minus 2 standard deviations and implies the process must be watched carefully if average or range points fall in this zone. The Green zone is plus or minus three standard deviations where most of the points for the average and range should fall. Data in this area indicates the process is in control and should be left alone as everything is OK. (See Figure 14.10).

FIGURE 14.9 - Statistical Quality Control Record and Data Form

Product ____________ Size of Container ____________ Code ________ Plant ________

Sample	Frequency Of Sample Sets By Day For Line 4											
Number	7am	8am	9am	10am	11am	Noon	1pm	2pm	3pm	4pm	$\overline{\overline{X}}$	$\overline{R}$
1	18.5	15.3	16.3	19.1	18.7	15.9	16.8	16.0	16.0	16.1		
2	17.0	15.3	14.8	18.4	18.3	15.2	15.8	16.1	16.2	16.0		
3	16.5	18.4	14.6	18.6	17.7	14.8	16.4	16.3	16.5	16.0		
4	16.8	15.0	15.1	16.1	16.2	14.1	15.8	16.0	16.1	16.1		
5	15.0	15.0	15.0	17.5	17.9	15.4	14.9	16.2	16.0	16.2		
Sum of X Values	83.3	78.9	75.8	89.7	88.8	75.4	79.7	80.6	80.8	80.4		
$\overline{X}$	16.8	15.8	15.2	17.9	17.8	15.1	15.9	16.1	16.2	16.1	16.29	
R	3.5	3.4	1.7	3.0	2.5	1.8	1.9	0.3	0.5	0.2		1.88

Note 1:
$UCL_{\overline{X}}$ (Upper control limit for average) = $\overline{\overline{X}} + A_2\overline{R}$
$LCL_{\overline{X}}$ (Lower control limit for average) = $\overline{\overline{X}} - A_2\overline{R}$
UCL_R (Upper control limit for range) = $D_4\overline{R}$

Note 2:
A_2 for five (5) sample numbers in a set is equal to 0.58
D_4 for five (5) sample numbers in a set is equal to 2.11

FIGURE 14.9 - Statistical Quality Control Record and Data Form - Continued

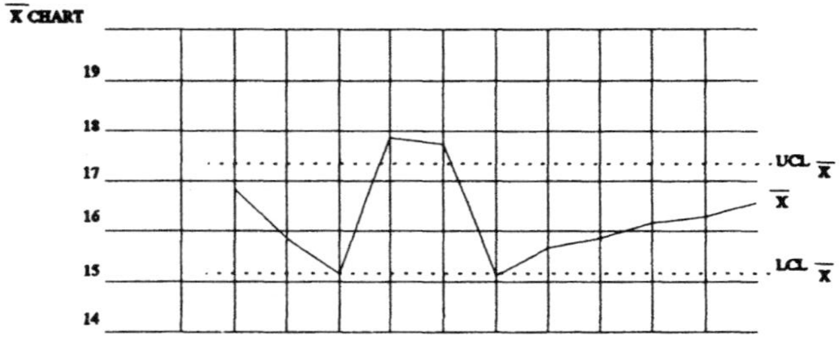

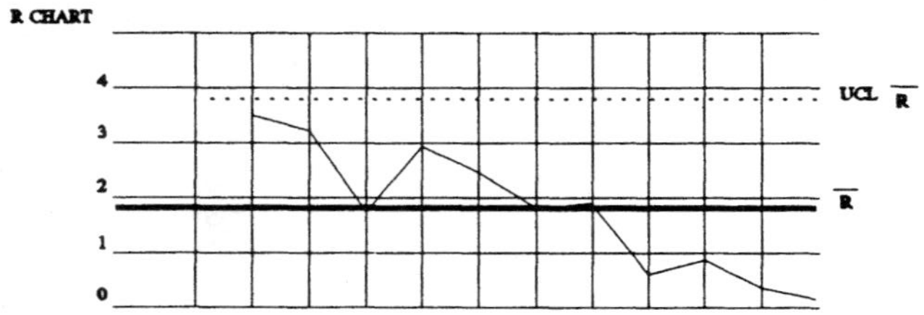

Run charts should be established for every unit operation in a process including incoming materials and outgoing products. It is a valuable history of the days operation and the operator who uses the chart will become much more efficient in producing uniform quality products.

FIGURE 14.10 - X Bar Chart Showing Zones For Control Charts

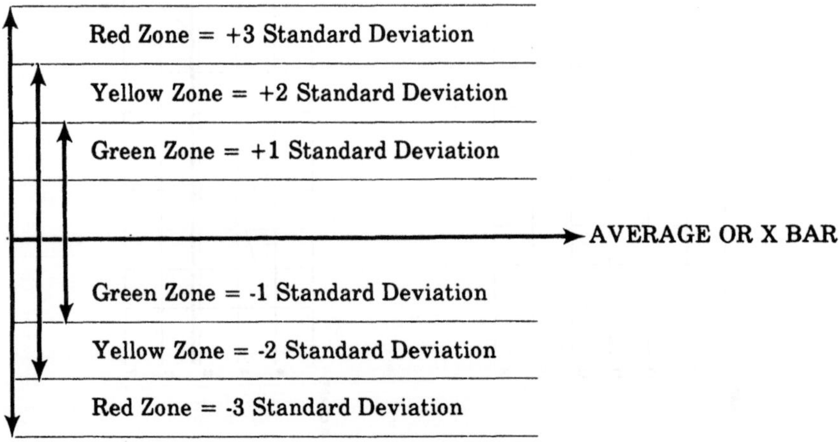

Red Zone = 68% of the Data
Yellow Zone = 96% of the Data
Green Zone = 99.7% of the Data

FIGURE 14.11 - Some Patterns Showing Types of Correlations

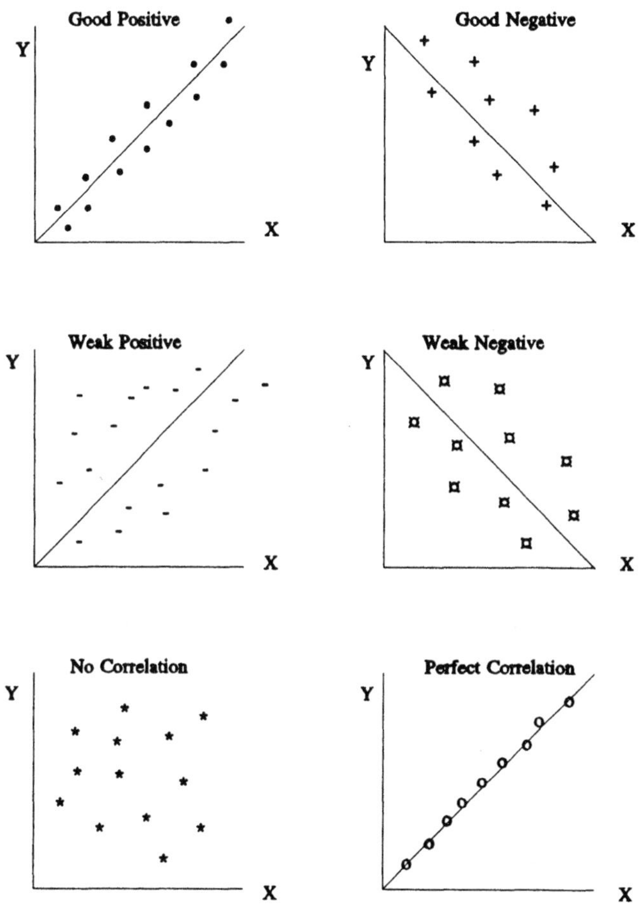

G. Scatter Diagrams And Correlation's - Problem Solving "Q" Tool No. 7.

Correlating data or charting is a tool to study how different variables relate to each other, that is, how they co-relate. This tool is used to test for possible cause and effect relationships.

The control variable (cause) should be plotted on the bottom or "X" axis (horizontal) of a graph and the measured variable (effect) should be plotted on the vertical or "Y" axis on the left hand side of the chart. The scale used on the chart should be appropriate to handle all the data and use up to least two/thirds of the graph paper available.

The correlation chart is used to study how different variables relate to each other. If one wanted to know if Line A was more efficient than Line B, or Machine A was easier to control over Machine B, or Ingredient A was an improvement over Ingredient B, the scatter diagram and correlation chart is the ideal way to study the data and make recommendations accordingly.

Whatever the problem, collect 50 to 100 pairs of samples of the data you wish to correlate. These numbers should be plotted on a chart. The completed data should show a pattern, that is, a scatter diagram of the relationships between the two variable (Figure 14.11). The relationship of the data may be better understood by drawing a line of best fit through the plotted points. If the scatter plots are all on the line, we say this is a perfect linear correlation. However, if the points are widely scattered, we call this a weak correlation or no correlation. A correlation may be positive if the two measured variables increase together. If one increases and the other decreases, this is a negative correlation.

Teams must collect data and they must use their "Q" tool box to become effective and reliable in their interpretation of what is actually happening to the process or the operation. Numbers (data) do not lie or exaggerate. Using actual data is a very simple method of keeping score. Numbers are your best source of telling you where you are and if you are winning. If you are a sports fan, you certainly want to know the score and you should feel the same way in your own operation. I am a big numbers person should be your attitude.

CHAPTER 15

COMMUNICATIONS

Thirty seconds can be enough time to make your point effectively if you plan properly. The proof is the 30-second television commercial.
The key is to always learn to focus on a single point.

All of us communicate in one way or another, that is, we talk, we listen, we see, we have body language, and we may touch. We communicate because we want to inform, control, solve problems, build teams, and help people to understand our position. "Good communication draws out of us an awareness of working together" (DePree). How effectively we communicate is the real test.

There are several basic steps to better communications. The first of these is being a better listener.

The Need To Listen

We need to listen with our ears and we need to really fully concentrate on what is being communicated.

We need to listen with our heart, that is, we must tune in to what is being communicated. We must follow the communicator and listen carefully and fully try to assimilate what is being communicated. In other words we need to pay attention and focus in on what is being communicated. When people do not listen to what is being said and they hear what they want to hear, valuable time is lost and perhaps the message that is being communicated is lost.

We need to listen with our hands and take notes to mentally remind us of what is being said. Note taking is a good sign that you are following and that you mean business about what is being said.

We may want to listen with our voice, that is, constantly restate or interpret what is being communicated. It may be necessary to ask the communicator to restate the message, that is, "is this what you meant?" or "have I got this right?". Yes, it may be necessary to ask other questions to clarify a given part of the message.

Finally, when we are listening, we should listen without our body language. Our posture and our gestures may be extremely upsetting to the communicator and it may indicate either concern or indifference.

Feeling

Another aspect of communication that is often overlooked is the feeling of the communicator. If the communicator is upset or has other matters on his mind, he most likely will not be concentrating on the message and it will interfere with a clear cut message. The communicator should be made to feel at ease and not up-tight over some matter that could be out of his control.

I have spent all of my adult life from serving in the Navy as an instructor to some 43 years as a Professor at The Ohio State University and now into my 40th year of working as an Executive with the food industry and the most frustrating aspect of working with people is having people attend a meeting that they do not care about. People that are forced to do something they could care less about take little interest and may be disruptive of all those others in attendance. Sometimes it is not their fault, but out of respect to the presenter, they should not choose this place to disrupt the others in the audience with their antics.

Keys To Communication

There are three keys to better communication. The first of these is that the communicator should learn to present only one idea at a time. Bombarding the listener with more than one idea will confuse many and the whole point of communicating will be lost.

The second key to better communication is not to monopolize the entire conversation. As one author states, when you turn your conversation into a monologue, you turn your listener(s) off.

The third key to better communication is to be explicit. Learn to say what you mean as precisely and as concisely as possible. The more specific you are, the better chance you have of being understood.

Experts tell us that there are ten principles of error-free communications to minimize communications problems:

1. Keep things simple. J. B. Priestly wrote, "the more elaborate our means of communications, the less we communicate".

2. Plan all your communications. List the important points you wish to make whether verbal or written communications and follow each point up.

3. Keep a copy of your communication documents for follow up discussions.

4. Do not ever assume your listener(s) understands what you tell them. Ask for questions to be certain they do and, if necessary, ask questions at length to clarify your position for the benefit of the listener.

5. Whenever and where ever possible use multiple approaches or methods to convey your message, with visuals, pictures, handouts, and reprints.

6. Do not rely on someone else to tell your story or give your message. Always do it yourself.

7. Learn to listen and observe your audience as they react to your message.

8. Never violate requests for confidentiality in regard to either personal or company information.

9. Keep written records and a file of discussions involving precedents and items that may be needed for later reference.

10. Always be as complete as possible rather than try to be brief.

Ways To Communicate

There are many ways we communicate with people. Some of these are as follows:

1. Hiring activities, that is, forms, announcements, interview practices, placement, etc.

2. Orientation, that is, personal handbook, benefit brochure, lockers, rest areas, floor plan, process lines, quality, teams, etc.

3. Policies and Procedure Manual

4. Training Manual(s)

5. House Organ

6. Bulletin Boards

7. Safety Handbook and MSDS data book along with policies on safety, clothing, etc.

8. Questionnaires, suggestion box, and survey forms.

9. Reports from teams, leaders, union, etc.

10. Annual Review(s), that is, how am I doing, am I making progress, what is my future, am I performing properly, etc.

The key to communications is that we need to learn how to send and receive messages. The sender simulates meaning in the mind of the receiver by means of a message conveyed using symbols of many types, and the receiver responds either mentally or physically to the message.

The sender in any communication process might be an individual, group, team, committee, or even the entire firm. The important part of any communication is a follow up or feed back. Our response is the best indicator that we have sent a message and the receiver is alert to it. The response may not always be what one expects, but, at least, the receiver heard the message and is reacting to it and that is the essence of communication. It is an ever ending process, but a must process to understand, comprehend, and react to the communication.

Ideally all messages or communication efforts should be in writing for the receiver to study and follow-up. Written messages take time and they must be short and concise, but written messages are less likely to be misinterpreted than verbal messages. Written messages do prevent the "grapevine".

Lastly, and probably the most important point about any communication is that it must motivate the receiver. The receiver needs to link up to the message and see the "window" that has been opened. It may be the opportunity the receiver has been looking for.

Communication is absolutely essential if a firm wishes to grow and understand itself, its customers, and its people. It should never be an after thought. It must be up front, complete, concise, and always timely. All formal presentations must be delivered in a manner that the receiver comes away with new knowledge, new insights, new beliefs, and new attitudes. Hopefully, the receiver becomes more enthusiastic, more enlightened, more understanding, and more a team player.

Success is achieved by taking one step at a time. Communication should be that first step for building a successful business and strong relationships with all concerned.

CHAPTER 16

BUILDING AN EFFECTIVE ORGANIZATION

You make people feel that they are with a special company, a special institution that's worth making sacrifices for. If you're the kind of person we call the "we and us" people that can work with the group by being unselfish, benefits will accrue to you by making sacrifices and if you're really good, you're going to get it back a hundred times. I think you have to get that point across. If you have pride in your organization you can get people to do anything. - Joe Paterno

Parts Of An Organization

There are many parts to an effective organization. I like to call them my "M's" and "E", that is, management, money, materials, machinery, methods, marketing, manpower, and environment. Each of these are part of the whole and no one can be eliminated or set-aside for success. I am only addressing the People issue in this discussion, in other words, your employees.

People

First, and foremost, a firm must obtain qualified people for each position in your firm. You must know the strengths and weaknesses of each person. You must have a detailed job description along with duties spelled out for each job in the firm and you must make certain every employee matches this as closely as possible. You should utilize the persons education to ascertain if the employee can really do the work required. You need to know the performance of all your employees. You need to know details about each employees work experience. You should know whether or not your employee can do the physical work required or whether or not any employee has any physical impairment. There is a place for everyone and sometimes that place may not be with your firm. Careful interviewing is most significant in human relations development.

Train Them Well

Many people who are employed need additional training and most of us need re-training. With all the sophisticated equipment starting at the office end and running through the factory to the marketing side, we find new helpful equipment and devices coming to the forefront. It behooves a firm to investigate and utilize this equipment if it will improve the operation of the firm. Along with the new equipment, many people need refresher or re-training courses or workshops and/or up-dating seminars. In most re-fresher or re-training sessions there is something everyone can learn new by listening and applying the information to their job. However, the attendees must be willing to listen, to observe, and to participate to obtain the most from any re-fresher or re-training session.

Most of us have taken employment exams and asked to put round pegs in square holes and vice versa. The purpose of such tests is to find out if we are physically and mentally qualified to do certain work. This is most true in a food plant as some people cannot work around moving products on a production line, others may not be able to cope with high speeds, while others have difficulty with noise, etc. One must always put the right person in the right job at the right time. This may be easier said than done; however, we must always try. In many plants rotation of the worker is almost mandatory because of the type of work being done. Human resource managers should always put themselves in the workers position and one will quickly see the need for rotation or they may not find out that the individual is unable to do the work effectively.

Communicate To All

As previously stated any effective organization must have well developed communication. This starts with the Leader, the CEO/COO, and others in management. Employees need to know the mission, the vision, and the values of the food firm. They need to know what the firm believes in and they need to know how they view the customer. These views need to be ingrained into the minds and actions of every employee. They need to be their primary focus as they go about their work.

People need to believe that they are important. They must be willing to accept responsibility and authority and prove that they are capable of handling it. By keeping them informed on what is going on and confiding in them rather than let the grapevine develop, they will be much better employees. People will take much pride and show great enthusiasm when they share the limelight with their peers. They will take a stronger sincere interest in each other as they communicate through their teams. People want to be included and they want to be let in on what is going on. People need to be communicated with as they want to believe in the firm and what its mission, vision, and values are.

Do Unto Others As You Have Them Do Unto You

The most important part of any effective organization is the ability of the firm to help people succeed. People succeed because management lets them succeed. Management should empower them and constantly challenge them to greater heights. People grow as the firm grows and vice versa. People want challenges and they want to prove that they are capable of giving the expected performance. Thus, they become accountable for their actions and they make real contributions.

Lastly, and very important, is how we portray our feelings for a job well done. Everyone likes to be rewarded, recognized, and reinforced. We will discuss this subject in the next chapter. Suffice it to say here that a big "Thank You" is the starting place for any reward for good performance.

CHAPTER 17

REINFORCEMENTS, RECOGNITIONS AND REWARDS

Too much praise can be as counter productive as too little. Its best to praise what is specific and appropriate and offer it immediately after a task or project is completed.
Derkin & Wise.

Being sensitive and recognized for an honest effort is a most humbling experience. To bring out the best in people, one should be certain that successful performance is rewarded soon after the accomplishment. This is the ideal time and best way to reinforce their success and show their peers how valuable you think the effort was.

The leader should make the recognition or present the award and he should be as specific as possible about what it means to the team, the line, or the firm. A slap on the back to tell people you are doing a good job does not have much impact. Whenever possible, all recognition's and rewards should be made to the team and not the individual member to really build esprit de corp within the firm.

The whole idea of recognition or award is to bring out the best in your people. As far as possible all recognition's and rewards should be made in public view, such as, personnel gatherings or meetings.

Another significant point about recognition's and reward, always acknowledge every small success as a reason for a celebration. To the awardee, small success recognition's build much enthusiasm and willingness to strive harder.

As a follow up to all awards and recognition's, the leader should write a personal note to the recipient acknowledging their success. The leader should, also, notify the supervisor of his message through a blind copy or verbally and he should follow up with his personal note. In other words, the firm should make the most of the effort by the individual or the team. This will build morale and help others to seek higher levels.

Another technique that I found most valuable is a small gift or an invitation to a private luncheon. When cuff links were very fashionable, I can remember receiving different sets and I was deeply touched. I, also, remember giving luncheons to my co-workers to recognize their contributions. I, also, like the idea of the person or team of the month. I like the write-up in the firms' house organ. I like to see pictures of individuals in the press as they are recognized. I really believe in recognition's and rewards. In Figure 17.1 I have tabulated some examples of rewards and recognition's for effective contributions.

TABLE 17.1 - Examples Of Types And Kinds Of Rewards And Recognition's

Calling a person by 'first' name
Presentation of a company pin, brooch, tie tac/bar, ring, watch, bracelet, etc.
Invitation to social event, luncheon, or executive meeting
Named employee or team member of the month
Assigned a designated parking space for a period of time
Given a prize, such as, free trip, tickets to a play, etc.
Provided with the firm's jacket, cap, sweater, etc.
Allowed extra days off or opportunity to go on 'flex time'
Assignment of more responsibility and/or leadership role
Granted more freedom over goals of the firm
Put in charge of a future project
Opportunity to undertake training to increase competency in a given area
Given publicity throughout the organization for the accomplishment
Salary adjustment and or salary increase, stock option, bonus, or direct grant
New or better equipment, furnishings, books, or tools
Opportunity to visit with the Leader or President
Freedom to work on new projects or select new tasks
"Thank You".

CHAPTER 18

COMPETITIVE ADVANTAGE

We see things not as they are but as we are.

and

A leader succeeds or fails not so much because of what he does, but because of what he is able to get others to do. Good ideas are easier to come by than good implementation. People blindness kills careers. People sensitivity makes careers.

Competitive advantage in a business starts with the leader and his ability to lead. Generally it is the case of those firms that utilize all that is offered from Total Quality Management (TQM). Good leadership provides a food firm with quality materials to work with, with personnel who are happy and progressive and work together as a team, with processes that produce products that are highly acceptable all the time, and with services to the customers that are well beyond reproach. People want to be led. They do not want to be managed. Leaders should manage themselves and then lead the firm. Leaders are in great demand to assure the competitive advantage a firm must have.

The leader of the food firm recognizes the advantages of TQM and they should use many teams to help his firm stay competitive. The vision of the leader must be well beyond the direct concern of the stockholders and the assurance of favorable bottom line each quarter. A successful leader needs to be concerned about the short run, but he should not let it dominate his thinking and his dealing with his customers and his people. He must have long term vision and be concerned about continuous improvement in incoming and outgoing materials, the process, the package, his customers and his employees. The leader needs to understand that satisfied customers come about because of better products and services with few, if any, complaints.

The modern day leader needs to understand that the employees make the product and they can eliminate mistakes, improve efficiency with better through-put and increased productivity if empowered and supported.

Everyone knows the CEO is the leader of most firms. Everyone knows that the CEO has the authority to make it happen. Everyone knows the CEO has the right to make changes in materials, the operating parameters for each process, the products being processed in terms of quality, and the personnel. Everyone, also, knows that the inaction of the CEO turns the team off and they quickly loose touch or the significance of their goal. They no longer want to be winners.

Employees tend to emulate the CEO or the leader if he is positive, aggressive, willing to move the firm forward, and the desire to look to the future with wise wisdom for the complete satisfaction of the customer and his people. The leader is a most powerful person. As I stated earlier, he is the coach and most team players will follow their coach if the coach is a true leader.

There is no question that the leader has a tough assignment, but if he cannot lead by example and make things happen he should admit this and move over or make room for another leader with the desired talent, will, and drive to take over and make the needed improvements to move the firm forward.

A successful leader relies on teams for help, guidance, assistance, leadership, and action. Teams are the rightful backbone to the leader of a food firm. Teams can keep the food firm competitive if the leader will train them and empower them to bring forth the new innovative ideas.

These new and innovative ideas must add value to the products, they must improve quality, they must make the product more tastier, and they must enhance the nutritive value of the processed products for the firm to obtain the much needed of the processed products for the firm to obtain the much needed competitive advantage. It is not an easy task, but many firms are doing it today and they are surviving because they are on the cutting edge, they have the competitive advantage. They are making a name for themselves and they are creating a product that the customer wants.

CHAPTER 19

SELF EVALUATION

"Whosoever desires constant success must change his conduct with the times" - Nicolo Machiavelli, 1531

Self evaluation is a difficult task because no one really wants to know just how bad things really are. However, self evaluation is the smartest thing we should all do. Take a look at yourself in the morning and what do you see? This is the image you carry around all the time and its the image we all see. If it is a good one we have no problem; however, if it is not so good we may have to do other things to correct for the way we are. I heard a speaker one time say that we should take advantage of our disadvantages. There is a whole lot of truth in this and it could work to help some of us out.

Learning From The Past Efforts

We should all learn lessons when we complete a project or a phase of a given project. We should meet as a team and learn from our effort. We should use the following questions as we evaluate our effort and use these questions as a starting point and build as we go along:

What was successful with this study or project?

What failed and why did it fail?

Would we do differently if we could start over?

Can we apply information from this work to future programs or projects?

If the approach we used this time worked in the past, why didn't it work this time?

What was different this time?

How could it have been different?

Who authorized or made the change?

Craig Nathanson in Quality Progress (9/93) asked the following question: Are you a Quality Person? His goal was to see if you meet the total quality criteria. He wanted to see how you would rate yourself on the following three categories: Personal Leadership, Planning, and Improvement. I have reproduced his questions below. Answer each on a scale of 1 to 10 with 1 through 3 being "rarely", 4 through 7 meaning "sometimes", and 8 through 10 meaning "always".

Personal Leadership

1. I treat other people fair and with respect.

2. I actively listen to other people and don't interrupt to give my point of view.

3. I take responsibility for my actions and don't rely on others to plan my future.

4. I volunteer my services to help others in need.

5. I maintain a healthy, positive out look on life.

6. I understand my values and apply them in my daily living.

7. My long and short term goals are tied to my values to ensure that what I am doing in my life is important to me.

8. My daily activities are in harmony with my values.

9. I enjoy the people and things in my environment.

10. I practice good customer service with all the people with whom I come into contact.

Planning

11. Every day I take time to plan my daily activities around that which is important to me.

12. I try to align my long and short term goals with my values to ensure that my daily activities are in harmony with my goals.

13. During my daily planning time, I prioritize both important and routine activities that I need to accomplish.

14. Each day I plan to accomplish only those activities for which I have allocated enough time.

15. I strive for continuous learning and have plans to further my education in areas that interest me.

16. I strive to work up to the standards set by the most accomplished people in areas that interest me.

17. I try to exceed the expectations of all of the customers with whom I come into contact in my activities.

18. When I plan my activities, I have knowledge of my environment and take any changing elements in consideration.

19. I have a good sense of how my personal values, strengths, and weaknesses align with what I am doing.

20. I have thought out realistic goals with achievable targets for my major activities.

Improvement

21. I can document three major processes that I use in accomplishing my personal goals.

22. I constantly strive to improve my skills, knowledge, and sense of purpose in my life's work.

23. I constantly strive to measure whether I am meeting my personal goals.

24. I constantly strive to eliminate activities that have no value in my life and focus only on activities that enrich my life.

25. I admit my mistakes, acknowledge the reasons, and then move on with the goal to not make the same mistake again.

26. I celebrate my successes and improvements.

27. I measure my successes by achieving my goals on time.

28. I constantly strive to improve in areas that are important to me and learn to accept my weaknesses in areas that don't interest me.

29. I am a role model for continuous improvement in everything I do.

30. I am open to changes in my life that will enable me to learn new things.

Nathanson says if your total score is 60-89 (Grade F) you might want some of these individual total quality strategies to get your life back on track.

If you scored 90-128 (Grade D), you might want to analyze your daily living patterns and goals in life. You do not demonstrate an individual total quality philosophy.

If you scored 129-158 (Grade C), you demonstrate some patterns of a total quality person but need to be more constant on a daily basis.

If you scored 159-229 (Grade B), you have a good individual foundation in total quality principles and could serve as a role model for others.

Finally, if you scored 230-300 (Grade A) you are a great total quality role model, with a solid set of principles in leadership, planning, and continuous improvement.

Each of us may want something different out of life and we each should have our own agenda. However, when working together and as a member of a team, we need to forget our personal agenda and think of the team, its goal, and what we are working toward. It may not always be easy, but in the long run it is well worth while.

One derives much personal satisfaction in working with others who have the same goal and when the team wins, everyone is a winner. Its a great thrill to be a winner and a part of winning team effort.

CHAPTER 20

CONTINUOUS IMPROVEMENT

"One trait that characterizes the Baldridge Award recipients is that they realize that quality improvement is a never-ending process, it is a company wide effort in which every worker plays a critical part".
President Ronald Reagan

Success

Kevin Bowler stated that "Success is based on people, product, process and persistence". In the past we measured success by using a given Sigma level. Some firms were using as high as a 6-sigma level meaning that there were no more than 3.4 defects per million units. Most people today strive for a zero variance. Thus, employees must commit to high performance, uniform quality, and complete customer satisfaction.

Employees must remember that all quality starts with me. We are important in the success of our firm. We are the leaders of the change. We make the difference.

The most important aspect of zero variance is to always know where we are, thus, we should always use feedback. When we use feedback, we are letting our feelings come out and we experience them in light of what others are doing, that is, we are critiquing ourselves and our co-workers. Every individual in the firm must make a commitment to continually improve for progress to happen. Every individual must do the right thing the first time and at all times.

Ryan summarizes three criteria for winners as follows, "Leadership, Strategic Quality Planning, and Human Resource Utilization". The following is a summary of some key points he stresses under each category.

Leadership

"All members of top management teams are visible in establishing and attaining strategic quality goals. Top management maintains close and direct contact with their customers. A clear champion, cheer leader or coach is visible within the firm. Top management has clearly defined the concept of quality. Management places quality ahead of profits, market penetration, sales and stock prices. Management has proven that when quality goals are realized the other measures of a successful business are readily attained".

Strategic Quality Planning

"A formal quality planning function or process exists, is actually used, and is typically integrated into the business planning process. The planning process emphasizes continuous quality improvement. The quality planning process considers not just one year ahead, but extends well into the future".

Human Resource Utilization

"Essentially everyone in the organization is involved in the quality process. All understand the quality policy and basic elements of the quality process as applied to their part of the organization. A cultural change has taken place, harnessing energies of the entire organization to continually improve quality exists".

"Every winner of the Baldridge Award has placed strong emphasis on problem prevention rather than problem solving and sorting inspection. Further, process quality measures demonstrate effective control and indicate trends of continual improvement".

The secret of continuous improvement is that a firm does not wait until the firm is up against the wall--they search for a better way when times are good. Kettering once stated that "if we wait until we have to, its too late". I firmly believe this and

I believe in following the policy of the Deming Cycle, that is, Plan, Do, Check, and then Act as shown in Figure 20.1

Planning

Planning simply means that we go through at least, three steps: We analyze where we are. We plan where we would like to be, that is, we prioritize the things to do. We establish a goal, that is, the order in which we put our objectives and the time when they must be completed. This requires a lot of effort on the part of the individual, the team, and the leader. All plans must be in writing and all plans must be made known to all concerned.

To know where we are we must have facts, that is, facts or data about our productivity, our quality, our financial status, our people--their abilities, their background in terms of education and desires, their training, their current interest and their willingness to help the firm move forward, their personal expectations and the expectations of the team, and their interest in achieving the goal. People are the key when planning and all firms must recognize that this is the starting point in building for the future.

In planning, we also must have a short range and a long range plan and this requires much commitment on the part of the management of the firm. They must commit not only to their people, but to their process, their products, their customers, and their resources. Management must, also, declare their mission for being, their vision of where they are and where they want to be, and their declared values, that is, what do we really stand for. They must "walk the talk", that is, they must be visible and back up their stated values, and vision. They can no longer operate in a vacuum. They must set forth their views for all to see and, hopefully, understand their goal(s).

Do

Secondly, they must Do. Do simply means to implement the plan, that is, put the proposed changes into effect. This may take much time as people have to be brought along first and educating them to the new culture change or the new way requires time, resources, and many changes from "the old way" to "the new way" (See Figure 20.2).

Check

The third part of the Deming Cycle is to Check, that is, bench mark your firm against the best of the competition. This simply means two things: First, we evaluate the present process, the work of the people, the products they manufacture, and their productivity today. Secondly, we study and measure the best of our competitors who are recognized as the best industry leaders. We compare ourselves to the best and then make our move as to how to restructure and prepare to move forward.

Act

Lastly, we Act, that is, we implement the changes to improve our process, our products, our people, and our services. This may take some time, but if we start now we will win the race to improvement. We must understand that what was good enough yesterday will not be good enough in the future.

We should keep a record on various aspects of our firm and plot data as shown in Figure 20.3. This will show us where we are today and what could happen as we learn to be a superior firm by our performance. The more vertical your company line, the greater improvement you are showing. The key is to always inform your people how well we all are doing. Communication and reinforcement, and recognition are keys to continuous improvement. It is not an easy road to follow, but making continuous improvement is the right way to greater success.

By way of summary, I like to use the 5 "T's" when working with people.

Talk

First, one must learn to TALK with all the people in the firm. We need to tell them what we are all about. We need to communicate to them Our Mission, Our Vision, and Our Values. We need to share with them our aspirations as a firm, as a team, and as individuals. We need to always help them reach the goal. We need to keep them fully informed.

Train

Secondly, one must TRAIN them. We need to help them with people skills, with technical know how, and administrative skills, if needed. Training is something that we should do all the time. It is part of coaching, teaching, and leading. However, people need more than knowledge, they need know how and what is part of any sound training.

Team

Thirdly, we need to TEAM them, that is, we need to have people work together for the good of the whole. Teams need leadership, guidance, and always a goal. They need members that develop great chemistry together. They need to be involved and they need to work as one. Teams are the future of building a firm. James Lundy described TEAMS as follows: Together Each Achieves More Success. A very good way to encapsulate what we mean by teams.

Trust

My fourth "T" is TRUST. This simply means that we empower our people, our team, and each individual. We must always instill in them that empowerment means responsibility and accountability. Trust is what we all build on and it is what successful firms are made of. They have trust for their products, processes, procedures, and personnel who always give the customer what they expect all the time. Trust says to me that I will do my thing and more for the good of the firm and its future.

Thanks

My last "T" and probably the most important is to say THANKS. Thanking people for doing their thing is a simple means of reinforcement, recognition and a reward for something well done. It is the easiest thing to do, but we often forget about it and when we do we loose great respect as a leader and the individual or team losses enthusiasm, loyalty, and empathy for him, the firm, and its effort to show continuous improvement.

FIGURE 20.1 - The Deming Cycle

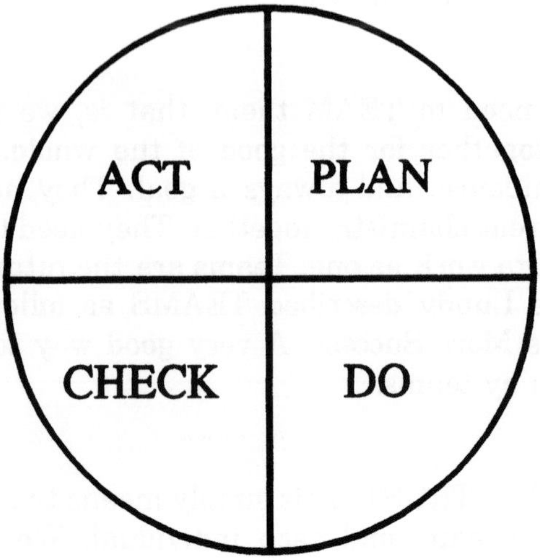

FIGURE 20.2 - The Old Way Verses The New Way
Some Modern Paradigm Shifts

The Old Way	The New Way
Accept all materials as delivered.	Establish specifications on all incoming materials and accept only those in compliance.
Employ "grab" sample system.	Use statistical sampling plans and sample accordingly.
Control of product quality by quality control personnel.	All production personnel trained in control practices and the application and use of Statistical Process Control (SPC).
Segregation of bad products from good products after processing.	Poor products are not produced because of prevention methods utilized in the manufacturing process.
Criticizing of employees for poor product quality.	Recognition of employees for any improvements in product quality
Employees receive little or no training for assigned task.	All employees working in the system are adequately trained for the task.
Employees have no say in the process.	Employees have a voice in the decision process.
Employees do what they can under the circumstances.	Employees do their job right because they have the proper direction, tools, knowledge, and the right environment.
Employees work according to the clock with little regard to process efficiency or product quality.	Employees develop pride and enthusiasm for the job and the products they produce.
Process whatever is delivered and evaluate the finished product and find a disposition for whatever the quality.	Measure the process capabilities and control the process to given specifications with predictions of product quality outcome.
Problems are solved by hit or miss practice.	Problems are solved by Pareto principle and use of Cause and Effect (CEDAC) charts.

FIGURE 20.2 - The Old Way Verses The New Way
Some Modern Paradigm Shifts - Continued

The Old Way	The New Way
Products are manufactured by "close enough" syndrome	Products are manufactured according to specifications and in conformation to label requirements.
Quality is controlled subjectively	Quality is controlled objectively.
Problems are always coming up - uncertain about quality.	Never have to say "I'am sorry" - always certain about quality.
Price of quality is nonconformanace- what it costs to do things wrong. (PONC).	Price of quality is conformance at all times - what it costs to get things done right the first time. (POC).
Vendors are unpredictable as to quality, delivery and price.	Vendors are rated on quality, delivery schedules, and price.
Management is not seen or available.	Management is by walking around (MBWA).
Quality is unpredictable - What you see is what you get.	Quality is planned and predictable - We know what to expect at all times.
Process of Detection.	Process of Prevention through HACCP.
Company receives complaints.	Company receives compliments.

FIGURE 20.3 - Are We Making Progress?

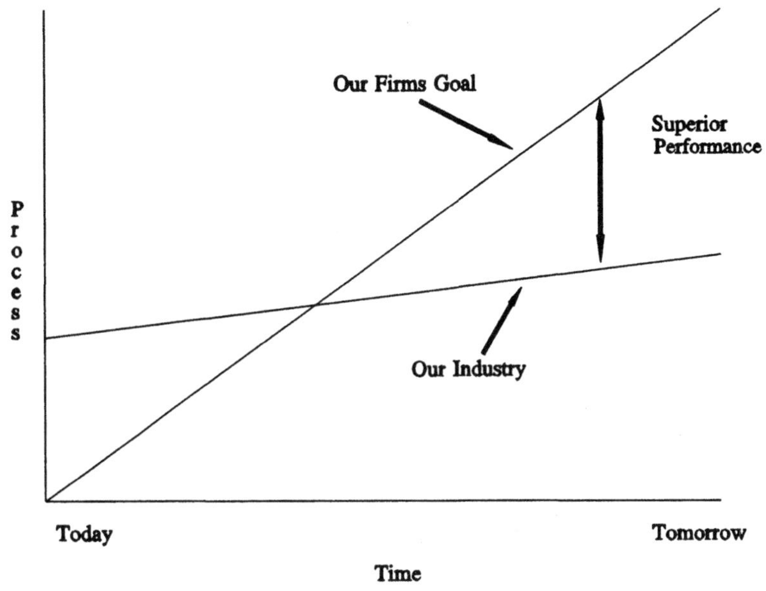

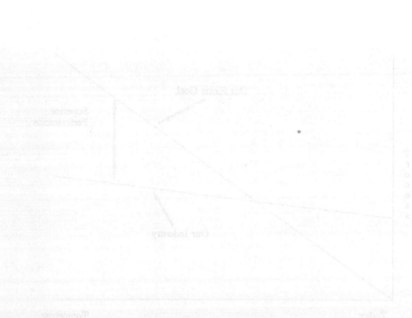

CHAPTER 21

SOME HIGHLIGHTS OF LABOR LAWS AND REGULATIONS

This Chapter prepared in cooperation with

STEVEN B. WHEELER
Human Resource Consultant
Wheeler & Associates
Phoenix, MD 21131

No attempt is made in this chapter to be all inclusive, but rather to highlight some of the major laws and regulations governing human resources in the workplace. The Human Resource Director should refer directly to the laws and regulations and should always seek advice of legal counsel on any and all labor matters.

Each Act or Regulation is highlighted as follows:

The Fair Labor Standards Act of 1938

As amended, covers minimum wages, overtime pay, equal pay for equal work, termination policies, and child labor standards. Prohibitions against age discrimination were added to the act in 1967.

On April 1, 1991 the Federal Minimum Wage is at least $4.25 per hour. Specific details dealing with exemptions, overtime pay, child labor, and training wages are described in the Act.

The following records must be maintained under this Act:

Employee's Name and Identification Number

Home Address

Birth Date if under 19

Sex and Occupation

Time of Day and Date Employee's Work Week Begins

Regular Hourly Rate of Pay

Hours Worked per Day and per Week

Total Weekly Earnings exclusive of Overtime Pay

Total Overtime Premium Earnings

Total Additions or Deductions from Pay

Total Wages Paid per Pay Period

Date Paid and Pay Period covered by Payment.

Details of the Act are available from the U. S. Department of Labor, Employment Standards Administration, Wage and Hour Division, Washington, DC 20210

The Occupational Safety and Health Act (OSHA) of 1970

Enacted to provide a means of reducing the ongoing incidence of illnesses and injuries caused by substandard safety and health conditions in the workplace. This Act covers all non-public employers including workplaces, offices, factories, yards, mills, and construction sites. Each covered employer is required to maintain the following records:

A log of workplace injuries resulting in death, lost time, restricted work capability, and/or medical treatment, or illness;

A supplemental report of each such illness or injury; and

The publication of annual summary of the log. The log must be "conspicuously" posted during the following February of each year.

OSHA and the Environmental Protection Agency (EPA) have a memorandum of understanding relative to chemicals in the workplace, hazardous disposal facilities and Superfund sites, MSDS program, asbestos regulation and required records in an effort to improve their efforts to protect workers, the public and the environment.

The Title III of the Superfund Amendments and Reauthorization Act (SARA) requires owners and operators of a facility to provide information to local government officials concerning large quantities of hazardous chemicals and any releases of hazardous chemicals into the environment. This is also known as the Right to Know law or provision which is designed to increase public knowledge and access to information regarding hazardous chemicals in the community.

Workers' Compensation

Each state has its own workers compensation statute with the intent of the system to obligate the employer to provide compensation and medical expenses for injured employees, regardless of fault, when they become disabled because of work-related injuries or illness. In exchange, the employer is given immunity from common-law suits brought by employees for work related injuries, so called negligence tort claims. Reporting on a Monthly and/or Quarterly basis with an Annual Report is mandatory in most states.

National Labor Relations Act: Union Organizing And Unfair Labor Practices.

The National Labor Relations Act (NLRA) is the single most comprehensive federal employment law regulating private-sector employers, unions and employees. The NLRA is not only the source of comprehensive rights and obligations applicable to employers, unions, and employees, but it also establishes the National Labor Relations Board (NLRB) to administer the law and settle disputes that arise under it. The NLRA preempts state laws and the rights and obligations imposed by the NLRA are generally decided by the NLRB, with only limited federal judicial review.

Drug Free Workplace Act, 1988

This Act applies to Federal Government contracts valued at more than $25,000 and to government grants of any value. The Act requires that employers do the following:

1. Publish a statement notifying employees that the unlawful manufacture, distribution, dispensation, possession or use of controlled substances is prohibited at the workplace. The statement must specify the range of disciplinary actions that may be taken against an employee for violation of this policy.

2. Establish a drug-free awareness program to inform employees about:
   a. The dangers of drug abuse in the workplace;
   b. The employers policy of maintaining a drug-free workplace;
   c. Any available drug counseling rehabilitation and employee assistance program; and
   d. The penalties that may be imposed upon employees for drug abuse violations.

3. Provide employees with a copy of the drug policy, which requires them to agree to abide by the policy and to notify the employer within five (5) days of any criminal drug statute conviction occurring in the workplace.

4. Notify the contracting government office of any employee drug conviction within ten (10) days of being notified thereof.

5. Require the convicted employee to undergo drug rehabilitation or discipline, which may include termination.

6. Make a good faith effort to maintain a drug-free workplace.

The act does not address the issue of drug testing programs, nor does it specify the type of discipline or sanction to be imposed on offending employees, leaving these matters to the discretion of the employer.

The penalty for non-compliance is the possible loss of government contracts or grants for up to five (5) years. Non-compliance occurs if there is:

1. False certification that a drug-free workplace is in effect;
2. Failure to comply with the drug-free workplace certification; or
3. The occurrence of a number of employee drug convictions in the workplace sufficient to indicate non-compliance with the certification.

Department of Defense Regulations

The regulations require a Department of Defense contractor to institute and maintain a program designed to achieve a drug-free work force. The contractor is free to design its own program, but the regulations suggest the following elements:

1. Employee assistance programs emphasizing education, counseling, rehabilitation and coordination with available community resources;
2. Supervisory training to identify and address employee drug abuse;

3. Provision for self and supervisory referrals for drug abuse problems;
4. Testing for employees in "sensitive" positions, which are defined as those employees:
    a. In positions having access to classified information;
    b. In positions involving national security, health or safety;
    c. In positions requiring a high degree of trust or confidence.

Although the Department of Defense regulations do not explicitly require random drug testing, DOD has stated that random testing is required to implement its regulations.

The DOD regulations suggest that an employer decide who to test by considering the following:

1. The nature of the work being performed under the contract;
2. The employee's duties;
3. The efficient use of contractor resources; and
4. The risk to public safety and security if the employee fails to perform his or her position because of drug use.

The regulations also suggest discretionary drug testing in the following circumstances:

1. When there is a reasonable suspicion that an employee uses illegal drugs;
2. When an employee has been involved in an accident or unsafe practice;
3. When it is part of or is a follow-up to counseling or rehabilitation for illegal drug use; and
4. As part of a voluntary employee drug testing program.

The regulations also indicate that an employer may establish a pre-employment testing program for applicants.

In addition to these basic substantive requirements, the Department of Defense regulations require a contractor to "adopt appropriate personnel procedures to deal with employees who are found to be using drugs illegally." If an employee in a "sensitive position" tests positive for drug use, then the regulations require the contractor to remove the employee from his position and prohibit him from returning to duty until the employee shows his ability to perform in a sensitive position according to the contractor's procedures.

The Federal Anti-Discrimination Laws

Include Title VII of the Civil Rights Act of 1964, the Civil Rights Acts of 1966 and 1971, the Age Discrimination in Employment Act, The Equal Pay Act, the Immigration Reform and Control Act of 1986, the Rehabilitation Act of 1973, and the Vietnam Era Veterans' Readjustment Allowance Act of 1974. In addition nearly every state has enacted laws prohibiting job discrimination on the basis of certain traits.

Human Resource personnel need to be well aware of all of these laws and follow the information provided in Chapter 7 on the New Employee dealing with questions and details of the hiring process.

Age Discrimination in Employment Act (ADEA) 1967

In 1986, Congress amended ADEA to prohibit age discrimination for those age forty (40) or over.

ADEA covers nearly all employers, except that an employer subject to ADEA must have at least 20 employees.

Employers may not use the age of a worker or applicant within the protected age group as grounds for:

- Failing or refusing to hire an individual
- Discriminating against employees with respect to their compensation or terms or conditions of employment.
- Bars employers from advertising any employment preference that discriminates against those within the protected age group.
- Limiting, segregating or classifying employees in any way that tends to deprive them of employment.

An employer's ADEA recordkeeping requirements include:

- Payroll records - containing each name, address, date of birth, pay rate, occupation and earnings.
- All personnel records pertaining to recruitment, hiring, promotion, demotion, transfer, lay off, recall training and overtime policies.
- Benefit plans and written seniority or merit rating systems.

Civil Rights Act of 1991

The Civil Rights Act of 1991 became effective November 21, 1991. This legislation expands the scope of existing employment discrimination laws, provides employees and former employees a jury trial in discrimination suits, and allows recovery of compensatory and punitive damages for violations of Title VII of the Civil Rights Act of 1964.

Some of the highlights of this Act will significantly affect the rights and liabilities of employers.

- Under prior Title VII guidelines an individual who prevailed with a discrimination suit could only receive lost wages benefits and attorney fees; Now they are eligible for compensatory and punitive damages.

The amount of compensatory and punitive damages is limited to:

$50,000 in a claim of an employer with 15-100 employees,
$100,000 in a claim of an employer with 101-200 employees,
$200,000 in a claim of an employer with 201-500 employees,
$300,000 in a claim of an employer with 500 or more employees.

- The jury trial provision is especially significant for employers. Since juries tend to be more driven by sympathy, are biased against "deep pocket" employers and are unpredictable, employers should expect to be adversely affected by this change.

Family Medical Leave Act

The Family and Medical Leave Act requires private, non-profit and government entities with 50 or more employees to provide eligible employees (employees who have worked for the employer at least one year and a minimum of 1,250 hours in the previous year) with up to 12 weeks of unpaid leave during a 12-month period under certain conditions.

Spouses employed by the same employer may be limited to a combined total of 12 weeks unpaid leave in a 12-month period for the purpose of birth or care of a baby, adoption, or care for a sick parent.

However, each spouse is entitled to up to 12 weeks' unpaid leave during any 12-month period for their own illness, or the serious health condition of a spouse or child.

Covered employers must provide up to 12 weeks of unpaid leave because of:

- The birth or placement for adoption or foster care of a child;
- A serious health condition of a spouse, son, daughter or parent;
- A serious health condition that makes the employee unable to perform the functions of his position.

Medical Certification

An employer can require a doctor's certification to validate an employee's serious illness.

Further, an employer can require a second medical opinion at his own expense, but the health care provider giving the second opinion cannot be a person who is regularly employed by the employer.

If the two medical opinions conflict, the employer may require, again at his own expense, that the employee obtain a third opinion from a health care provider approved by both. The third opinion will be final and binding.

Implications of Intermittent or Reduced Leave

An employer can require an employee who needs to take "intermittent" leave (for example, one work day off per week over a 15-week time span) to transfer to another position of equivalent pay and benefits while the employee is temporarily undergoing the planned medical treatments.

"Reduced" leave does not result in a reduction in the employee's total allowable leave time.

For instance, if a 40-hour-a-week employee takes leave at the rate of 20 hours per week (or half the normal work week), the leave will stretch over 24 weeks (or double the 12-week allowable leave).

Health Insurance Coverage Remains Intact

Though Family and Medical Leave may be unpaid, employers must continue the employee's health insurance at the same level and under the same conditions as would have been provided if the employee remained continuously employed.

Other Important Points

As part of the 12-week family leave, employees may be required to use accrued vacation or personal leave, or medical or sick leave, when the employee has a serious health condition.

This would encompass such traumatic conditions as heart attacks, severe nervous disorders and pregnancy-related conditions like miscarriage.

An employer can require 3 days' notice of foreseeable leaves for birth, adoption or planned medical treatment.

The act permits the employer to recover a health premium if the employee fails to return to work after the leave period has expired, or fails to return for a reason other than the continuation of a serious illness.

Once the law becomes effective, employers are required to continually post a notice of the provisions of the Family and Medical Leave Act of 1993 in a location highly visible to employees, as well as job applicants.

The Employee Retirement Income Security Act (ERISA)

The Employee Retirement Income Security Act of 1974, commonly referred to as ERISA, was enacted by Congress with the declared intent to protect the interests of participants in employee benefit plans and their beneficiaries by:

- requiring the disclosure and reporting of financial and other information,
- establishing standards of conduct and responsibility for fiduciaries of employee benefit plans, and
- providing for appropriate remedies, sanctions, and ready access to the federal courts.

ERISA applies to "employee welfare benefits plans" and to "employee pension benefit plans."

1. An Employee Welfare Benefit Plan is any plan, fund or program maintained by an employer or by an employee organization, or by both, for the purpose of providing for its participants and/or their beneficiaries, through the purchase of insurance or otherwise, any of the following types of benefits:
    - medical, surgical, or hospital care or benefits;
    - benefits in the event of sickness, accident, disability, death or unemployment;
    - vacation benefits, apprenticeship or other training programs; or
    - day care centers, scholarship funds, or prepaid legal services.

2. An Employee Pension Benefit Plan is any plan, fund, or program which is maintained by an employer or employee organization, or by both, that by its express terms or as a result of surrounding circumstances:
    - provides retirement income to employees, or
    - results in a deferral of income by employees until termination of employment.

3. The term Employee Pension Benefit Plan may encompass certain severance pay plans and tax sheltered annuity plans, but generally does not encompass individual retirement accounts or bonus programs.

4. Title I of ERISA (reporting and disclosure requirements) does not apply to:
   - governmental plans,
   - church plans,
   - unfunded excess benefit plans, and
   - plans maintained solely for the purpose of complying with applicable workman's compensation or disability insurance laws.

ERISA imposes certain liabilities and duties on persons exercising discretion or control over an employee plan

- Administrator
- Sponsor
- Employer
- Named Fiduciary
- Fiduciary
- Trustee
- Investment Manager
- Party of Interest
- Participant
- Beneficiary

Also, Basic Fiduciary Rules impose four standards

- The exclusive benefit rule
- The prudent new rule
- The diversification requirement, and
- The requirement of compliance with the plan provisions consistent with ERISA requirement.

Other areas are:

- Co-Fiduciary Liability
- Prohibited Transactions
- Participant Directed Investment plus duty of reporting and disclosure.
- Duty of Disclosure
- Specifics of the reporting and disclosure requirements
- Penalties for failure to comply with reporting and disclosure requirements.

Finally, Summary of Basic ERISA Documents:

- Plan Document and Trust
- Summary Plan Description
- Summary of Material Modifications
- Filing of Annual Form 5500
- Benefit Statements to Participants

The Americans With Disabilities Act of 1990 (ADA)

The Americans With Disabilities Act is a federal civil rights statute designed to address the claims and concerns of Americans who are of working age with a disability. The Act bans both discrimination in employment and discrimination in "public accommodation" (i.e., physical facilities used by the public). ADA provisions covers all employers with 15 or more employees.

Some covered employment practices are:

- Job Application Procedures
- The Hiring or Discharge of Employees
- Employee Compensation
- Advancement
- Job Training
- Other Terms, Conditions and Employment Privileges.

Also, ADA prohibits

- Discrimination against a "qualified individual with a disability".
- Most medical examinations and inquiries about disabilities, and
- Retaliation against anyone who has exercised rights under the Act

Who is Disabled?

Any individual is subject to a disabling condition within the meaning of the Act if he or she:

- has a physical or mental impairment that substantially limits one or more of a person's major life activities, or
- has a record of such an impairment, or
- is regarded as having such an impairment.

Reasonable Accommodation

- Includes any accommodation that the employer can make without "undue hardship".

Other examples include:

- The alteration of physical facilities so employees with disabilities can get to their work areas.
- Changes in work procedures to facilitate the performance of the essential functions of jobs
- The reorganization of work duties among a group of employees
- Modification of work schedules and waiver of leave/ attendance policies

The employment provisions of the law will be enforced by the EEOC.

Vocational Rehabilitation Act of 1973

The Rehabilitation Act, which prohibits employment discrimination based on a handicap against persons otherwise qualified to perform a job, does not apply to private employers. However, all federal contractors and any recipient of federally financed assistance is now considered to be a public employer for purposes of the Act.

The federal definition of a disabled individual has three elements. The disabled person:

1. Has a physical or mental impairment that substantially limits one or more major life activities.
2. Has a record of such an impairment, or
3. Is regarded as having such impairment.

If an employee or job applicant meets one of these three definitions, he or she is in the protected group.

Older Workers Benefits Protection Act (OWBPA)

In 1990, Congress passed OWBPA. This legislation was passed in response to a Supreme Court decision, the outcome of which outraged many Congressmen and segments of their constituencies. The Court held that ADEA (Age Discrimination in Employment Act) did not forbid age discrimination in the area of employee benefits, except in unusual circumstances.

OWBPA rejects the Supreme Court's controversial decision by defining "compensation, terms, conditions or privileges of employment" as including employee benefits, even those provided under a bona fide employee benefit plan. Consequently, Section 4 (a)(1) of ADEA now forbids discrimination in employee benefits, as well as in every other aspect of employment that is not protected by some specific exception from coverage of the Act.

Immigration Reform and Control Act of 1986

The Immigration Reform and Control Act of 1986 (IRCA) has three main purposes:

1. Provide a solution for controlling illegal immigration to the United States;
2. Make limited changes in the system for legal immigration; and
3. Provide a controlled legalization program for undocumented aliens who entered the United States prior to 1982.

IRCA altered several immigration provisions of the Immigration and Naturalization Act of 1952.

First, a new immigrant category for dependents of employees of international organizations was created. IRCA recognized the unique position of children and spouses of long-term international organization employees when those employees die, transfer or retire. It is often difficult for children and spouses to become oriented to their original society and culture. For all purposes.

These individuals are "Americanized". The special immigrant category recognizes their Americanization and allows the individuals to remain in this country if they meet certain residence requirements.

Second, IRCA restricts the ability of many foreign students to adjust their status to that of lawful permanent resident aliens. This modification was aimed at reducing the number of foreign students who remain in the United States. IRCA also altered the allocation of visas and created a visa waiver program.

Finally, IRCA modified the former H-2 program for temporary workers by adding the H-2A program for temporary agricultural workers. It also established a mechanism by which special agriculture workers are admitted to perform field work in perishable crops. Under this section, agriculture workers move freely between employers without penalty and are fully protected under all federal, state and local labor laws.

This change allows a legal labor pool without reducing the available workers to harvest perishable crops.

The employer and employee must fill out an Immigration and Naturalization Service (INS) form called I-9. The I-9 form doesn't require that copies of the documentation be retained, but the employer may make copies and keep them on record.

Important

Because IRCA limits the uses to which the I-9 forms and backup documents can be used, employers may keep such information in a <u>separate</u> file from other employee personnel files to avoid any claim of their improper use by law-enforcement agencies or the employer.

Consolidated Omnibus Budget Reconciliation Act (COBRA)

An employer that employs 20 or more persons on a typical business day and maintains a group health plan is required to provide continuation of coverage. Under COBRA legislation, the definition of "employee" can include an independent contractor.

A "qualifying event" is any event that would normally result in a loss of coverage for the covered employee or qualified beneficiary were it not for the application of COBRA. These events are:

- The death of the covered employee;
- The termination (other than by reason of gross misconduct) or reduction of hours of the covered employee's employment;
- Divorce or legal separation;
- The covered employee's becoming entitled to Medicare benefits;

- A dependent child ceasing to meet dependency requirements, or
- A proceeding in a case under federal bankruptcy law with respect to the employer from whose employment the covered employee retired at any time.

Generally, coverage must last at least 36 months. However, the coverage must last 18 months for reduction of hours or termination of employment. If a second qualifying event occurs before expiration of this 18 month period, the period is extended to 36 months.

Also, the employer is required to give written notice of COBRA rights to the employee and their spouse. With other qualifying events like:

- Dependency status of a child,
- Divorce,
- Legal separation,

The employer is required to give notice to the plan administrator within 30 days of the event. If in the event of divorce, legal separation or when a child ceases to be a dependent, the covered employee or qualified beneficiary must notify the plan administrator within 60 days of such event. Within 14 days of receipt of that notice, the plan administrator must notify the covered employee and/or qualified beneficiary of their COBRA rights.

Worker Adjustment and Retraining Notification Act ("WARN")

The Worker Adjustment and Retraining Notification Act ("WARN"), requires employers to give employees, or their exclusive collective bargaining representative, and certain government officials 60 days prior notice of a plant closing or mass layoff. Litigation under WARN is helping to clarify and define the scope of an employer's obligation under the law.

The threshold question under WARN is whether a business enterprise constitutes an "employer." "Employer" is defined as:

Any business enterprise that employs-

(a) 100 or more employees, excluding part-time employees; or

(b) 100 or more employees (including part-time employees) who in the aggregate work at least 4,000 hours per week (exclusive of hours of overtime).

In determining whether the employing entity meets the definition standard, workers temporarily laid off or on leave, if they have a "reasonable expectation or recall," and temporary workers must be counted.

The term "employer" includes non-profit organizations, but excludes regular federal, state and local governments and federally recognized Indian tribal governments. Public and quasi-public entities may be "employers" if the entity engages in "business," is organized separately from the regular government, and has its own governing body with independent management authority.

The determination of whether a subsidiary or independent contractor is a separate employer from the parent or contracting company depends on the two entities' independence from each other. That determination involves consideration of the following factors: (a) common ownership, (b) common directors and/or officers, (c) defacto exercise of control, (d) unity of personnel policies emanating from a common source, and (e) the dependency of operations.

Two circumstances trigger an employer's requirements to give notice - a plant closing and a mass layoff.

1. Plant Closing
    - Shutdown
    - Facility or Operating Unit
    - Single Site of Employment
    - Employment Loss
2. Mass Layoffs
    - A reduction in force which
      (a) is not the result of a plant closing; and
      (b) results in an employment loss at the single site of employment during any 30 day period for at least 33% of the active employees (excluding part time); and at least 50 employees (excluding any part-time employees), or at least 500 employees (excluding any part-time employees).

Generally, notice is required at least 60 calendar days before the scheduled plant closing or mass layoff.

Exceptions to the 60-Day Notice Requirement:

- Faltering company
- Unforeseeable business circumstances
- National Disaster
- Extension of layoff

Exemption from Warn Notice Requirement:

- Temporary Employment
- Strike or Lockout

The Equal Pay Act

The equal pay act states that male and female employees who perform the same work for the same employers must receive the same rate of pay.

There are several exceptions. An employer may pay one employee more than another for the same work based on greater productivity or seniority. Also, if a company has more than one facility and its operations are in different labor markets, wages can vary to reflect labor supply and demand.

The comparable-worth theory attempts to expend the coverage of the Equal Pay Act. The Equal Pay Act requires that male and female worker doing the same job for the same company and location must, if all else is equal, receive the same pay. Comparable worth enthusiasts compare different job classifications to other, unrelated, classifications to determine whether each job group is of equal worth and, if so, equally compensated.

There are, also, laws dealing with AIDS in the workplace, Pregnancy and Maternity leave, Polygraph Protection Act, etc.

Sources of official information should come direct from congress, U. S. Department of Labor, EPA, OSHA, and trade associations, such as, National Food Processors Association, The Snack Food Association, and, of course, the legal fraternity.

CHAPTER 22

HUMAN RESOURCE ACRONYMS

This Chapter prepared by

STEVEN B. WHEELER
Human Resource Consultant
Wheeler & Associates
Phoenix, MD 21131

Many of us use acronyms in our everyday language when discussing various issues. To assist us in understanding the Human Resource language, we have provided a list for your future usage. Of course, this list will continually have to be added to in the future.

Keys

---

[1] = Employee Relations
[2] = Benefits
[3] = Safety
[4] = Equal Employment Opportunity
[5] = Compensation
[6] = Health
[7] = Labor

The keys correspond to the various Human Resource functions.

AAA	- American Arbitration Association [7]
AACP	- Affirmative Action Compliance Program [4]
ADA	- Americans With Disabilities Act [4]
ADEA	- Age Discrimination in Employment Act [4]
ADR	- Alternative Dispute Resolution [1]
AIDS	- Acquired Immune Deficiency Syndrome [6]
ALJ	- Administrative Law Judge [7]
ARC	- Aids Related Complex [6]
BFOQ	- Bona-Fide Occupational Qualification [4]
CDC	- Centers for Disease Control [6]
COBRA	- Consolidated Omnibus Budget Reconciliation Act [2]
DFWA	- Drug Free Workplace Act [1]
DOD	- Department of Defense [1]
DOJ	- Department of Justice [1]
DOL	- Department of Labor [7]
DOT	- Department of Transportation [3]
EAP	- Employee Assistance Plan [1]
EEOC	- Equal Employment Opportunity Commission [4]
EPA	- Environmental Protection Agency [6]
EPA	- Equal Pay Act [5]
ERISA	- Employee Retirement Income Security Act [2]
ESOP	- Employee Stock Ownership Plans [2]
FLSA	- Fair Labor Standard Act [5]
FMCS	- Federal Mediation and Conciliation Service [3]
FMCSR	- Federal Motor Carrier Safety Regulations [3]
FUTA	- Federal Unemployment Tax [5]
IRA	- Individual Retirement Plans [2]
IRCA	- Immigration Reform and Control Act [1]
LMRA	- Labor-Management Relations Act [7]
HAZMAT	- Hazardous Materials [3]
HIV	- Human Immune Deficiency Virus [6]
HMO	- Health Maintenance Organization [2]
NIOSH	- National Institute of Occupational Safety & Health [3]
NLRA	- National Labor Relations Act [7]
NLRB	- National Labor Relations Board [7]
NRC	- Nuclear Regulatory Commission [1]
MESA	- Mining Enforcement Safety Administration [3]

MSDS	- Material Safety Data Sheet [3]
MSHA	- Mining Safety and Health Administration [3]
OFCCP	- Office of Federal Contract Compliance Programs [4]
OSHA	- Occupational Safety & Health Act [3]
OSHRC	- Occupational Safety and Health Review Commission [3]
OWBPA	- Older Workers Benefits Protection Act [2]
PBGC	- Pension Benefit Guaranty Corporation[2]
PPO	- Preferred Provider Organization [2]
RTK	- Right to Know [3]
SEP	- Simplified Employee Pensions [2]
TITLE VII	- Civil Rights Act of 1964 [4]
VDT	- Video Display Terminal [6]
WARN	- Worker Adjustment and Retraining Notification [1]

While this list is representative of those acronyms associated with the Human Resource field, it's not a comprehensive or all-inclusive list.

REFERENCES AND FURTHER READINGS

Blanchard, K. et al 1990. *The One Minute Manager Builds High Performing Teams.* Wm. Morrow & Co., Inc. NY, NY

Fournier, F. F. 1978. *Coaching for Improved Work Performance.* Liberty Hall Press, McGraw Hill, Inc. NY, NY

Goldratt, E. M. & Robert E. Fox 1986. *The Race.* N. River Press, Croton on the Hudson, Hudson, NY

Gould, Wilbur A. 1992. *Total Quality Management for the Food Industries.* CTI Publications, Baltimore, MD.

Gould, Wilbur A. and Ronald W. Gould. 1993 *Total Quality Assurance for the Food Industries.* CTI Publications, Baltimore, MD.

Kinlaw, D. C. 1991. *Developing Superior Work Teams.* Lexington Books, Lexington, MA

Miller, James 1993. *The Corporate Coach.* St. Martin's Press. NY, NY

Miller Lawrence M. 1991. *Design for Total Quality - A Workbook for Socio-Technical Design.* Miller Consulting Group, Inc., Atlanta, GA.

Miller, Lawrence M. and J. Howard. 1991. *Managing Quality Through Teams - A Workbook for Team Leaders & Members.* Miller Consulting Group, Atlanta, GA.

Osburn, J. D. et al 1990. *Self Directed Work Teams: The New American Challenge.* Business One Irwin, Homewood, IL.

Quick, Thomas L. 1992. *Successful Team Building.* Amacon, A. Division of American Management Association, 135 W. 50th St. NY, NY

Ryan, John 1989. *The Hare and the Tortise Revisited.* American Society for Quality Control, Milwaukee, WI

Shonk, James H. 1992. *Team Based Organizations.* Business One Irwin, Homewood, IL.

Thomas, Brian 1992. *Team Quality Training. The Quality Culture and Quality Trainer.* McGraw Hill Book Co., NY, NY

Winchell, Wm. 1991. *Continuous Quality Improvement.* A Manufacturing Professional's Guide. Society of Manufacturing Engineers. Dearborn, MI.

INDEX

FIGURE INDEX

NOTES

NOTES

NOTES

NOTES

Printed and bound by CPI Group (UK) Ltd, Croydon, CR0 4YY

08/05/2025

01864830-0003